Joint Commission
on Mental Illness and Health

MONOGRAPH SERIES / NO. I

Current Concepts of Positive Mental Health

MARIE JAHODA

A REPORT TO THE STAFF DIRECTOR, JACK R. EWALT
1958

Basic Books, Inc., Publishers, New York

Foreword

THIS IS the first of a series of monographs to be published by the Joint Commission on Mental Illness and Health as part of a national mental health survey that will culminate in a final report containing findings and recommendations for a national mental health program.

The present document constitutes a report of the project director to the staff director of the Joint Commission.

Titles of the monograph series, together with the senior authors, are listed here in the approximate order of scheduled publication:

1. *Current Concepts of Positive Mental Health*
   Marie Jahoda, Ph.D.

2. *Economics of Mental Illness*
   Rashi Fein, Ph.D.

3. *Mental Health Manpower*
   George W. Albee, Ph.D.

4. *Nationwide Sampling Survey of People's Mental Health*
   Angus Campbell, Ph.D., and Gerald Gurin, Ph.D.

5. *The Role of Schools in Mental Health*
   Wesley Allinsmith, Ph.D., and George W. Goethals, Ed.D.

6. *Research Resources in Mental Health*
   William F. Soskin, Ph.D.

7. *Religion in Mental Health*
   Richard V. McCann, Ph.D.

8. *Nonpsychiatric Community Resources in Mental Health*
   Reginald Robinson, Ph.D., David F. DeMarche, Ph.D., and Mildred K. Wagle, M.S.S.A.

9. *Epidemiology and Etiology of Mental Illness*
   Richard J. Plunkett, M.D., and John E. Gordon, M.D.

10. *Patterns of Patient Care:*
    A. THE OUT-PATIENT
    B. THE IN-PATIENT
    C. THE EX-PATIENT
    Morris S. Schwartz, Ph.D., Warren T. Vaughan, M.D., and Charlotte Greene Schwartz, M.A.

These monographs, each a part of an over-all study design, will contain the detailed information forming the basis of a final report. From the data in the individual studies and other relevant information, the headquarters staff will prepare a summary document incorporating its findings and recommendations for national and state mental health programs. This summary document will have the approval of the Joint Commission before its publication in the form of an official report.

This final report will be published by Basic Books and transmitted to the United States Congress, the Surgeon General of the Public Health Service, and the Governors of the States, together with their representatives in the public health and mental health professions, in accordance with the provisions of the Mental Health Study Act of 1955.

Participating organizations, members, and officers of the Joint Commission, as well as headquarters and project staffs, are listed in the appendix at the end of the book.

The Joint Commission, it may be seen, is a nongovernmental, multidisciplinary, nonprofit organization representing a variety of national agencies concerned with mental health. Its study was authorized by a unanimous resolution of Congress and is financed by grants from the National Institute of Mental Health and from private sources.

Additional copies of *Current Concepts of Positive Mental Health* may be obtained from the Joint Commission headquarters, from the publisher, or from book dealers.

JOINT COMMISSION ON MENTAL ILLNESS AND HEALTH

Staff Review

THE NEED for a clearer understanding of what we mean by "mental health" is obvious to anyone who has attempted to cope with the role of schools and the numerous community agencies involved in mental health promotion, prevention of mental illness, and other phases of the mental health movement now in progress in the United States. Any possible clarification of the subject should be of help to mental health program-makers.

We commonly use "mental health" as a term interchangeable with "mental illness," in the same euphemistic way that "public health" generally refers to the prevention or control of disease by mass methods. The behavioral scientists who have joined the mental health team and are making increasingly important contributions to the mental health movement have expressed dissatisfaction with a primary focus on "sick behavior." They argue that a new and broader perspective is needed if interest in mental health, as a positive force, is to be made conceptually clear and practically useful. They make a telling point when they propose that progress in understanding health and illness requires much research based on the study of human behavior as a natural phenomenon.

In approaching the subject of this monograph, we have thought primarily of the promotion of mental health as a positive state, rather than of the cure of mental illness, or its prevention.

We asked Dr. Marie Jahoda, the author, who is Professor of Social Psychology, New York University, and Director of the N.Y.U. Research Center for Human Relations, to conduct a review of the pertinent literature and also hold an interdisciplinary seminar during the academic year 1956–57 for the purpose of evaluating the theoretical, experimental, and empirical evidence of the psychological nature of mental health.

Dr. Jahoda's fulfillment of this assignment has resulted in a thoughtful and extensive analysis of mental health concepts, written by her in consultation with leading public health workers, sociologists, psychologists, and others.

No abstract can take the place of the total document—a process of critical examination of existing views and issues and of where they lead. However, it may be helpful to have a summary of some of the prominent features of her report. These points are made, among others:

1. Mental health is an individual and personal matter. It involves a living human organism or, more precisely, the condition of an individual human mind. A social environment or culture may be conducive either to sickness or health, but the quality produced is characteristic only of a person; therefore, it is improper to speak of a "sick society" or a "sick community."

2. In speaking of a person's mental health, it is advisable to distinguish between attributes and actions. The individual may be classified as more or less healthy in a long-term

CURRENT CONCEPTS
OF POSITIVE MENTAL HEALTH

view of his behavior or, in other words, according to his enduring attributes. Or, his actions may be regarded as more or less healthy—that is, appropriate—from the viewpoint of single, immediate, short-term situation.

3. Standards of mentally healthy, or normal, behavior vary with the time, place, culture, and expectations of the social group. In short, different peoples have different standards.

4. Mental health is one of many human values; it should not be regarded as the ultimate good in itself.

5. No completely acceptable, all-inclusive concept exists for physical health or physical illness, and, likewise, none exists for mental health or mental illness. A national program against mental illness and for mental health does not depend on acceptance of a single definition and need not await it.

6. Many scientific investigators have thought about the psychological content of positive mental health. A review of their contributions reveals six major approaches to the subject.

a. Attitudes of the individual toward himself.

b. Degree to which person realizes his potentialities through action.

c. Unification of function in the individual's personality.

d. Individual's degree of independence of social influences.

e. How the individual sees the world around him.

f. Ability to take life as it comes and master it.

7. One value in American culture compatible with most approaches to a definition of positive mental health appears to be this: An individual should be able to stand on his own two feet without making undue demands or impositions on others.

8. The need for more intensive scientific research in mental health is underscored.

Among the biologists and physicians who read this monograph, there may be some discomfort at not finding more about the biologic and physiologic components of mental health. They might even take their cue from the fact that Dr. Jahoda states that "mental health must be thought of as pertaining to a living organism with mental faculties." However, it is the purpose of her monograph to discuss the concepts of positive mental health from a psychological viewpoint. She assumes that a certain physiologic or physiochemical homeostasis is necessary for good health.

The laboratory showed us long ago that severe emotional stress can profoundly alter the physiology of the body. More recent research supports this evidence—chemical-physiologic disturbances can affect behavior and perception. In fact, some evidence indicates that a genetic, or at least fundamentally biologic, "set" of the body, in terms of its chemical constituents, may determine the way the individual deals with external stress and other life experiences.

In addition, deterioration of the brain from disease, aging, nutritional disturbances, or toxins such as alcohol and drugs can produce profound mental changes. Adequate nutrition and maintenance of a high state of oxygenation of the fetus during delivery and in the immediate post-partum phase may, in themselves, promote a better integrated nervous system and a higher state of mental health in the future.

For those who contend that mental health is a unitary state to which all must conform, it may be pointed out that Dr. Jahoda suggests that good physical health is a necessary but not sufficient condition of good mental health.

Some, however, feel that mental health is a more relative term. For example, they believe that mental health would be possible in a genius and a moron as well. They may contend that a person with a brain injury who has recovered with only a few neurologic disturbances can, in spite of this, with proper rehabilitation and proper mental attitudes, have good mental health. Speculation almost requires such a point of view, else, from a biologic point of view, we could never be certain that any man is healthy. Who knows what ordinary mortals among us might have been an Einstein or Edison, had a few more cubic centimeters of oxygen been infused into our lungs, or had our mothers ingested a few more vitamins or particular constellations of protein during our gestation period?

None knows that he is as intact as he might have been. Perhaps the biologic view would be adequately represented if, to Dr. Jahoda's psychological concepts and notions of mental health, were merely added a phrase—"with a physiologic function consistent with the demands made by the society and the psychologic state of the individual."

The final chapter in this monograph was written by Dr. Walter E. Barton, one of the members of Dr. Jahoda's advisory panel, in order to present what might be termed a more typical clinical view of the organic facets in this problem. This staff review, Dr. Jahoda's presentation, and Dr. Barton's all help confirm Dr. Jahoda's contention that mental health indeed means different things to different people.

JACK R. EWALT, M.D., *Director*

Acknowledgements

THIS REPORT was written for the Joint Commission on Mental Illness and Health. The Director of the Commission, Dr. Jack R. Ewalt, and his senior staff, particularly Drs. Fillmore H. Sanford and Gordon W. Blackwell, did much more than entrust me with a piece of work; their continuous encouragement, and the generous and thoughtful manner in which they permitted me to enlist the cooperation of others, have been of considerable help.

Work on this report was planned and carried through in a manner which required several revisions of ideas, formulations, and organization. When a preliminary draft of a section was finished, it was first submitted to my colleagues at New York University for criticism and suggestions. Drs. Robert R. Holt, Murray Horwitz, George S. Klein, Robert S. Lee, Eva Rosenfeld, M. Brewster Smith (Vice-President of the Joint Commission), Miss Claire Selltiz, and especially Drs. Isidor Chein and Stuart W. Cook gave their time and ideas unsparingly. Their individual contributions cannot be identified. Jointly they made it possible to produce interim working papers which led to an immeasurable improvement of the draft they had received from me. These working papers were then submitted to a highly selected group of professional persons who acted as consultants to the project. They are as follows:

Alfred L. Baldwin, Ph.D., Professor and Chairman of the Department of Child Development and Family Relationships, Cornell University, Ithaca, N. Y.

Walter E. Barton, M.D., Associate Professor of Psychiatry, Boston University School of Medicine, and Superintendent, Boston State Hospital, Boston, Mass.

Kenneth D. Benne, Ph.D., Professor of Human Relations, Boston University, Boston, Mass.

John A. Clausen, Ph.D., Chief of the Laboratory of Socio-Environmental Studies of the National Institute of Mental Health, Bethesda, Md.

Ernest M. Gruenberg, M.D., Technical Staff, Milbank Memorial Fund, New York.

Irving L. Janis, Ph.D., Associate Professor of Psychology, Yale University, New Haven, Conn.

Ernst Kris, Ph.D., Clinical Professor of Psychology, Child Study Center, Yale University, New Haven, Conn. (Now deceased).

Lionel Trilling, Ph.D., Professor of English, Columbia University, New York.

After having studied the working paper, the consultants met with me for a meeting lasting about five hours. These seminars were also attended by Drs. Chein and Smith. All participants agreed that these meetings should serve as springboards for ideas and advanced criticism. The notion that intellectual efforts can be furthered by consensus or majority opinion was explicitly ruled out. The ensuing spirited discussions greatly enriched my knowledge and thinking about mental health.

Throughout the period of work on this report I had the competent and enthusiastic help of Mrs. Lillian Robbins and Mr. Nicholas Freydberg who, under the modest title of graduate student assistants, helped in every way, from taking notes at the meetings with consultants (much more economically and intelligently than a tape recorder could have done), to reading, excerpting, and discussing. In the final revision and organization of the report, Mrs. Robbins and I worked closely together. Miss Mary Insinna coped gracefully and efficiently with the secretarial duties inherent in the task.

To all of them my warm thanks.

MARIE JAHODA

Contents

THERE ARE two ways of being interested in health; the common one is that of making a list and plan of all things that are good and desirable in life and giving the best possible description of Utopia and of perfection with recommendations as to how to get there. The way of the worker in modern hygiene is that of making a survey of the actual activities and conditions, and then of taking up definite points of difficulty, tracing them to an understanding in terms of causes and effects and to factors on which fruitful experimental, analytical and constructive work can be done. The first type leads mainly to moralizing; the second type leads to a conscientious and impartial study, and to constructive experimentation.

ADOLF MEYER, 1925.

I

Introduction

THERE IS hardly a term in current psychological thought as vague, elusive, and ambiguous as the term "mental health." That it means many things to many people is bad enough. That many people use it without even attempting to specify the idiosyncratic meaning the term has for them makes the situation worse, both for those who wish to promote mental health and for those who wish to introduce concern with mental health into systematic psychological theory and research.

PURPOSE AND SCOPE

The purpose of this review is to clarify a variety of efforts to give meaning to this vague notion. In doing so we shall have to examine the assumptions about the nature of man and society underlying such efforts by making explicit some of their implications and consequences. This should lead first to a description of various types of human behavior called mentally healthy and second to a critical discussion of mental health concepts suggested in the literature.

[3]

Definitions of mental health to some extent must be matters of convenience. A definition in itself solves no problems and does not add to knowledge; all that can be expected from it is usefulness in achieving the purposes of science. Yet, as we shall see, there are many efforts to define mental health in ways that go far beyond this scientific approach to definition. They often contain implicitly personal or general philosophies—they often specify how human beings ought to be. Such "definitions" also will have to be examined.

In a sense, the attempts to give meaning to the idea of mental health are efforts to grapple with the nature of man as he ought to or could be. Every historical period probably has its own characteristic way of searching for expressions incorporating its ideals of a good man in a good society. In our time and in this country positive mental health is one focus for this search. Why this should be the case would be an interesting study in itself. Here we must limit ourselves to noting that the inevitable closeness of ideas about mental health to fundamental values should temper scientific impatience with concepts that do not immediately suggest to the reader how they can enter into theoretical or practical work.

Since our goal is the development of a rational approach to the problem of defining mental health, we shall have to choose what seems best among those definitions intermingling value and fact. In sorting unnecessary from necessary connotations, and in indicating where necessary elements are still lacking, we will aim at definitions useful for both research and application.

IS A CONCEPT OF MENTAL HEALTH
NECESSARY?

Whether we like it or not, the term mental health, or mental hygiene, is firmly established in the thought and actions of several groups: First, under the guidance of voluntary and governmental agencies, the public has taken hold of the term in spite of (or, perhaps, because of) its ambiguity. Funds are being raised and expended to promote mental health; educational campaigns are being conducted to teach people how to attain this goal for themselves, for their children, for the community. But is there substance behind the notion? Can a useful concept of mental health be established?

If substance can be lent to the term, the effort will benefit the public, even if mental health emerges as less of a panacea than the public would like. From this situation, a moral obligation to deal with the matter arises.

Specialists also use the term mental health, particularly those professions trying to help people in trouble or to prevent them from getting into trouble. Thoughtful members of these groups feel that they need clarity about the concept of mental health because they want to use it to define realistic goals for their efforts and as a help in the development of techniques that, in application, will lead to these goals. It is the business of science to explore human potentialities and the conditions furthering their realization. The helping professions often turn to the behavioral sciences, therefore, to provide them with basic knowledge about human functioning. They demand a mental health concept compatible with scientific knowledge of man.

Finally, the term mental health is used by scientists themselves (such as psychiatrists, psychologists, sociologists, and anthropologists). Their concern with mental health is often justified by pointing to what appears to be a one-sided development in the sciences of man. Knowledge about deviations, illness, and malfunctioning far exceeds knowledge of healthy functioning. Even apart from the issue of application, they maintain, science requires that the previous concentration on the study of inappropriate functioning be corrected by greater emphasis on appropriate functioning, if for no other reason than to test such assumptions as that health and illness are different only in degree.

Other members of the scientific community oppose scientific concern with mental health. In part such opposition is based on an unwillingness to work with a notion so vague and ill-defined. In part it is rooted in the conviction that the science of behavior advances best by studying behavior, without reference to whether it is "good" or "bad." Only in this manner, they argue, can science remain free from "contamination by values" and a resulting distortion in the choice and study of scientific problems.

This argument rests upon the implicit assumption that as a rule scientists select the topic of their interests in accordance with the rational requirements of the discipline within which they work. This does happen, of course; a well-developed theory is, on occasion, the only guide to the choice of a research topic. But the very one-sidedness of current psychological knowledge testifies to the fact that, in their choice of topics, scientists are responsive to social demands being made of them. Whether psychological theory will benefit more by correcting an earlier bias in favor of the study of disease through a current bias in favor of the study of health, or by a strict avoidance of concern with "good" or "bad," healthy or sick functioning, is a matter of strategy. Fortunately, both strategies are presently being pursued by different people. Only the future will tell which was more profitable.

In any case, it does not detract from the value of a piece of work if it is chosen for other than theoretical reasons. Alexander Leighton (1949) has incisively stated the place of values in the science of man:

Within an area marked off for scientific investigation, the values of science reign supreme over each step in the process toward conclusions and in the conclusions themselves. Moral values when pertinent dominate scientific values at three contiguous points: the selection of the problem to be investigated, the limitation of the human and other materials that may be used, and the determination of what shall be done with the results.

From this point of view, mental health is a *possible* concern for scientific inquiry notwithstanding its value connotations. Earlier we argued that mental health is a needed concept, and one that can be given clear meaning only by scientific work. Perhaps it is best to let the argument rest here. Whether or not an individual scientist wants to engage in research related to mental health is up to him.

THE NATURE OF MENTAL HEALTH
PROPOSITIONS

It may be helpful in appraising the following review of concepts to keep in mind that one has the option of defining mental health in at least one of two ways: as a *relatively constant and enduring function of personality,* leading to predictable differences in behavior and feelings depending on the stresses and strains of the situations in which a person finds himself; or as a *momentary function of personality and situation.*

Looking at mental health in the first way will lead to a classification of individuals as more or less healthy; looking at it in the second way, will lead to a classification of actions as more or less healthy. The relevance of this distinction can be illustrated with an example concerning physical health. Take a strong man with a bad cold. According to the first, he is healthy; according to the second, he is sick. Both statements are justifiable and useful. But utter confusion will result if either of these correct diagnoses is made in the wrong context—that is, if he is regarded as a permanently sick person or as one who is functioning healthily. Much of the confusion in the area of mental health stems from the failure to establish whether one is talking about mental health as an enduring attribute of a person or as a momentary attribute of functioning. In the following discussion, we shall keep the distinction in mind without at this moment choosing between either position.

In the mental health literature a third type of statement occurs frequently: situations or societies are called healthy or sick. The German culture under national-socialist domination has been called paranoid; totalitarian systems are often regarded as unhealthy in democracies; one of Fromm's recent books bears the title *The Sane Society* (1955).

On closer examination, however, all these examples (and many other possible ones) present merely a linguistic trap in the discussion of mental health. To call a situation healthy or unhealthy is nothing but a colloquial ellipsis meaning that it is *conducive* to healthy or unhealthy behavior. In other words, mental health must be thought of as pertaining to a living organism with mental faculties; it cannot be attributed to any other entity.

This is, of course, not to say that the examination of aspects of a situation conducive to mentally healthy or unhealthy behavior is irrelevant. On the contrary: it is of the greatest importance, as will become clear in a later section. In the present context, however, where we are concerned with establishing the premises upon which mental health criteria can be established, the discussion of the situation is super-fluous. The relation of environment to mental health—in other words, the *conditions* under which a person acquires enduring mental health or will act in a mentally healthy way—must be postponed until the legitimate meaning, if any, of mental health as an attribute of human behavior has been explored.

II

Clearing the Air:
Unsuitable Conceptualizations of
Positive Mental Health

MENTAL HEALTH as the opposite of mental disease is perhaps the most widespread and apparently simplest attempt at definition. To accept this approach presupposes a definition of mental disease. Notwithstanding the fact that mental disease is at present much better understood than mental health, efforts to define mental disease meet with considerable difficulties.

THE ABSENCE OF MENTAL DISEASE
AS A CRITERION FOR MENTAL HEALTH

At the present stage of our knowledge, mental disease in many cases cannot be inferred from physiological changes in the functioning of the organism. When psychiatrists agree among themselves that they are dealing with a mentally sick person, they use as the basis for inference highly complex behavior patterns whose physiological correlates are usually not known.

When a person has lost "contact with reality," hallucinates, or is completely unable or unwilling to perform essential functions for survival, general agreement is quickly achieved. But there are many mentally ill persons who do not (at least not consistently) show such extreme symptoms. Here, diagnosis is not nearly as unanimous. On the other hand, there are situations in which apparently healthy persons may show one or several of these severe symptoms. Whether or not to call such persons sick will depend on whether the classification is made in terms of enduring personality attributes or in terms of currently observed actions.

To make explicit all the criteria leading to the diagnosis of disease is a baffling task. By and large, practitioners prefer to think in terms of personality attributes, whereas classification of actions has proved more useful in many research efforts. This question was debated in a Milbank Fund symposium (1953). Definitions of the following kind were reported: "A case is a person under the care of a psychiatrist"; or, with reference to children, "a 'case' is a child about whom the schoolteacher says, 'This child's behavior is not like most children's. The child is making trouble or having trouble.' "

These crude rule-of-thumb definitions actually served a purpose for research; at least they permitted it to get off the ground. But those who used these definitions were ready to admit severe limitations. For instance, probably many very sick people are not under the care of a psychiatrist; also, a much higher rate of mental disease was implied in communities having a psychiatrist than elsewhere. These definitions were adopted not out of a lack of sophistication, certainly, but in the realization that they provided an expedient way of starting research. The suggestion was also made that in our present state of knowledge a comprehensive concept of mental disease was perhaps premature.

Such self-critical restraint on the part of people well-qualified to define mental disease receives much support from anthropological studies. Some of these throw doubt on the use of some symptoms for the diagnosis of disease.

Anthropologists tell us of generally accepted behavior in some cultures that Western civilization would regard as symptomatic of mental disease. According to Ruth Benedict (1934), the Kwakiutl Indians of British Columbia engage in behavior that is, by our standards, paranoid and megalomaniacal. Their view of the world is similar to a delusion of grandeur in our culture. Alexander interprets the Buddhistic self-absorption of mystics in India, with its physical manifestations of rigidity and immobility, as an artificial schizophrenia of the catatonic type (Klineberg, 1954). However, it is apparently true that the Buddhist can control the onset and end of his "symptoms," a feat the schizophrenic person in our culture cannot perform.

The example suggests that similarities in symptoms must not be mistaken for identical disturbances of functions. It also illustrates—and this is important here—that whereas identical observable symptoms are regarded in one culture as achievement, in another they are regarded as a severe debility. In our culture, adolescent boys who are exposed to homosexual advances often take this as a sign that there is something fundamentally wrong with them. In some cultures, the *absence* of a homosexual approach is interpreted in the same fashion. Examples could be multiplied to indicate that the

*evaluation of actions as sick, or normal, or extraordinary in
a positive sense often depends largely on accepted social con-
ventions.*

Some anthropologists, however, have taken a strong stand
against cultural relativism in the identification of mental
disease. Devereux (1956), for example, argues that the
shaman is mentally sick, even though his illness takes a
culturally approved form. Linton's idea of culturally prescribed "patterns of misconduct" points in the same direction.
The fact that there are in various cultures different "proper
ways to be insane" need not imply that the functional disturbance in itself varies from culture to culture. Only with
regard to the manifestations of the disease is cultural relativism appropriate.

Devereux bases his argument on psychoanalytic theory,
thinking of mental disease as the expression of conflicts in
the unconscious. But it has not yet been demonstrated that
there are any human beings who are free from unconscious
conflicts. If it is reasonable to assume that such conflicts are
universal, we are all sick in different degrees. Actually, the
difference between anyone and a psychotic may lie in the
way he handles his conflicts and in the appearance or lack
of certain symptoms. If this is so, mental disease must inevitably be inferred from behavior. But, apart from extremes,
there is no agreement on the types of behavior which it is
reasonable to call "sick."

The differential evaluation of symptoms is not limited to
cross-cultural comparisons. Within our society, a farmers'
community may well regard as symptoms of mental disorder the behavior of, say, an urban artists' colony. It follows,
then, that human behavior cannot be understood in terms of

isolated symptoms but must rather be viewed in conjunction with the social norms and values of the community in which the symptoms are observed (Asch, 1952). Whether empirical and theoretical work on mental disorder will one day result in the identification of certain disturbances regarded as "disease" in all known cultures is as yet an open question.

Furthermore, the borderline between what is regarded as normal and as abnormal is dim and ill-defined in all but the extreme cases. Character disorders of various types, for example, belong to that large area where the label "mental disease" is not much more appropriate than that of the label "mental health," unless we can discover more rigorous criteria for one or the other than are implied by the current usage of these terms.

In discussions of these complex issues, a daring thought has recently been put forward that makes the definition of psychological health as the absence of mental disease even more doubtful. Such a definition is based on the assumption that health is the opposite of disease, or that health and disease form the extreme poles of a continuum. What if this assumption should turn out to be unjustified and misleading? Some psychiatrists now speak of different health potentials in seemingly equally sick patients, as if they were dealing with two qualitatively different continua. We shall return to this idea later on.

At this moment, however, the apparent difficulty in clearly circumscribing the notion of mental disease makes it unlikely that the concept of mental health can be usefully defined by identifying it with the absence of disease. It would seem, consequently, to be more fruitful to tackle the concept of mental health in its more positive connotation, noting, however, that the absence of disease may constitute a necessary, but not a sufficient, criterion for mental health.

NORMALITY AS A CRITERION FOR MENTAL HEALTH

As far as normality is concerned, what has been learned from cultural anthropologists can hardly be overestimated. Their entire work can be regarded as a series of variations on the theme of the plasticity of human nature and, accordingly, on the vast range of what can be regarded as normal. They have convincingly demonstrated a great variety of social norms and institutions in different cultures in different parts of the world; and that in different cultures different forms of behavior are regarded as normal.

It is generally accepted that the term normality covers two different concepts: normality as a *statistical* frequency concept and normality as a normative idea of how people ought to function. In the statistical sense of the term it is correct to say, for example, that normal adults are married. Whether or not the statement makes sense in the normative connotation is another matter. It may well be that for this example there is a coincidence of statistical and normative correctness. But such coincidence would be fortuitous. To believe that the two connotations always coincide leads to the assertion that whatever exists in the majority of cases is right by virtue of its existence. The failure to keep the two connotations of normality separate leads straight back into an extreme cultural relativism according to which the storm trooper, for example, must be considered as the prototype of integrative adjustment in Nazi culture.

Insofar as normality is used in the normative sense, it is a synonym for mental health, and the problems of concept definition are, of course, identical.

It remains to be seen what can be learned from the frequency concept. Implicitly, if not explicitly, many persons regard what the majority of people feel, think, and do as healthy, and deviations from the average as not healthy. This belief is fostered by the unquestionable fact that, with regard to many human attributes, the distribution of the population follows a normal or approximately normal curve; that is, the majority manifests a medium course, with progressively smaller proportions of cases as we move toward either extreme of behavior. This is true, for instance, for many biological functions (height, weight, and so forth).

However, a majority does many things we hesitate to call mentally healthy; for example, experiments have indicated that under conditions of hunger, people tend to see food where there is none. That the majority may respond in such fashion would perhaps be perfectly understandable; but this is different from regarding as psychologically abnormal those who, in spite of their hunger, maintain the ability to perceive correctly, because they are at the extreme end of this particular distribution curve. Psychological health may, but need not, be the status of the majority of people.

Moreover, statistical definitions of psychological health involve basically nonstatistical considerations. As Ernest Jones (1942) has pointed out, "If once the statistically normal mind is accepted as being synonymous with the psychologically healthy mind (that is, the mind in which the full capacities are available for use), a standard is set up which has a most fallacious appearance of objectivity." Davis (1938), Wegrocki (1939), Mowrer (1948), and Redlich (1952) also deal with the concept of statistical normalcy.

In order to establish a statistical norm, one has to define the population from which it is to be derived. And the choice of a population inevitably contains, at least implicitly, a non-statistical concept of health. One would not, for example, develop a set of statistical norms for an arbitrarily merged population including both so-called primitive and civilized societies, males and females, children and adults. Why not? Because it seems evident that the determining conditions of the same behaviors, the contexts, their consequences, and hence their meanings, to either the actors or observers, are often likely to be quite different in different types of society, or in the two sex groups, or in different age groups. It follows that in deciding upon a reference population, one is at least tacitly considering the determinants, contexts, consequences, and/or meanings of behavior relevant to its evaluation from the viewpoint of mental health.

Similarly, even when one has selected and defined the relevant reference population, one would not give equal weight to all measurable psychological functions—say, the speed with which a person can cancel all of the *a*'s in a page of print, on the one hand, and the frequency of hallucinatory experiences, on the other—in developing a set of norms against which to evaluate the mental health status of individuals. For it seems clear that, whatever "mental health" may mean, not all psychological functions are equally relevant to it. We thus again find that some, at least tacit, nonstatistical considerations must precede the application of the statistical approach.

The concept does not offer us any clues as to how to select and define a reference population or how to select and weight the psychological functions to be measured in an effort to evaluate *positive* mental health. If and when more appropriate criteria are discovered, their frequency distribution in any population will become an interesting empirical question. But as a criterion in itself, normality is of no use.

VARIOUS STATES OF WELL-BEING AS CRITERIA FOR MENTAL HEALTH

Many persons think of psychological health as manifested in a state of well-being. The World Health Organization, for example, defines health as "the presence of physical and emotional well-being." In this phrase written for international audiences, the term "emotional well-being" is but another label for mental health. Without a specification of what is meant by it, the phrase is of little help for our purposes.

Others have specified various criteria for an individual's different feeling-states. Karl Menninger (1947), for example, says:

Let us define mental health as the adjustment of human beings to the world and to each other with a maximum of effectiveness and happiness. Not just efficiency, or just contentment—or the grace of obeying the rules of the game cheerfully. It is all of these together. It is the ability to maintain an even temper, an alert intelligence, socially considerate behavior, and a happy disposition. This, I think, is a healthy mind.

This description contains a variety of criteria. Recognizing that we are not dealing with the full overtones and connotations in Menninger's rich language, it is reasonable for purposes of classification to select from his description, first, the terms happiness and contentment; they have wide currency as criteria of mental health. Menninger actually also assumes "that the unhappy are always (at least partly) 'wrong' "! To regard the unhappy as wrong or sick was apparently already prevalent about 1500 B.C., when the friends of Job told him that the reasons for his utter misery must be sought in himself.

Jones (1942) also talks of happiness as a criterion of normality. Others prefer the term "satisfaction." Boehm (1955), for example, writes: *"Mental health is a condition and level of social functioning which is socially acceptable and personally satisfying."*

In an informal inquiry conducted by the director of the Joint Commission on Mental Illness and Health to ascertain the meaning attached to mental health by a group of experts, a fair number described their ideas in terms of happiness, well-being, and contentment. There are obvious differences in degrees and quality among these various highly desirable states of being. To distinguish among them is, however, a minor matter compared to a major problem inherent in all efforts to regard various states of well-being as criteria for mental health. This difficulty has to do with the tacit assumption that happiness or contentment need no special referent or qualification.

In this global sense, people are happy if what they want from life is in harmony with what life offers. Such happiness is clearly not only a function of the individual but also of the course of external events over which the individual has no control. The use of unqualified euphoric states as criteria of mental health leads to a difficulty perhaps most obvious in Boehm's concept of mental health: What if social acceptability and personal satisfaction are incompatible? What if happiness or well-being, satisfaction or contentment, freedom from conflict or tension is inappropriate in a life situation? Do individuals then have to be considered mentally unhealthy? To answer this question in the affirmative betrays a naïve belief in the moral justice of all existing conditions.

But obviously, the persons quoted above are not naïve. Their formulations make it clear that they mean to speak in terms of more or less enduring personality attributes. Thus Menninger speaks not only of happiness but of a happy disposition. And Jones, in recognizing the impact of external events on the degree of happiness a human being experiences, is compelled to define happiness in a highly idiosyncratic fashion as the ability to hold impulses in check, without renouncing them, until they can be gratified. To regard the *unhappy disposition* as a criterion of poor mental health is one thing. To regard *unhappiness,* regardless of the circumstances in which it occurs, as such an indication is a different matter.

To be sure, to some extent man selects and creates his own environment, and to that extent even the unqualified term "happiness" appears as a possible criterion. But there are many facets of the environment beyond the conscious or unconscious choice and creation of the individual. Misfortune and deprivation are not necessarily of our own making. To be happy under such conditions cannot seriously be regarded as a criterion for mental health. Only when happiness or well-being are clearly conceived of as personality predispositions, rather than as momentary feeling states depending on circumstances, do these criteria appear useful. In this connotation they will enter into the subsequent discussion.

III

The Psychological Meaning of Various Criteria for Positive Mental Health

So FAR, three efforts to give psychological meaning to the notion of positive mental health have been examined and found more or less wanting. To regard the absence of mental disease as a criterion has proved to be an insufficient indication in view of the difficulty of defining disease. Normality, in one connotation, is but a synonym for mental health; in another sense it was found to be unspecific and bare of psychological content. Various states of well-being proved unsuitable because they reflect not only individual functioning but also external circumstances.

A survey of the relevant literature reveals a host of other approaches to the subject which seem more promising; at least, at first sight, it appears that the objections raised in the preceding pages do not apply to them. Although no claim can be made that this survey discovered every contribution to the topic, the search was extensive. It is hoped that no major idea in the area has escaped our attention.

SIX APPROACHES TO A CONCEPT

From an inspection of the diverse approaches uncovered, six major categories of concepts emerge.

1. There are several proposals suggesting that indicators of positive mental health should be sought in the *attitudes of an individual toward his own self*. Various distinctions in the manner of perceiving oneself are regarded as demonstrating higher or lower degrees of health.

2. Another group of criteria designates the individual's style and degree of *growth, development, or self-actualization* as expressions of mental health. This group of criteria, in contrast to the first, is concerned not with self-perception but with what a person does with his self over a period of time.

3. Various proposals place the emphasis on a central synthesizing psychological function, incorporating some of the suggested criteria defined in (1) and (2) above. This function will here be called *integration*.

The following three groups of criteria concentrate more exclusively than the preceding ones on the individual's relation to reality.

4. *Autonomy* singles out the individual's degree of independence from social influences as most revealing of the state of his mental health.

5. A number of proposals suggest that mental health is manifested in the adequacy of an individual's *perception of reality*.

6. Finally, there are suggestions that *environmental mastery* be regarded as a criterion for mental health.

All ideas on positive mental health examined can be assigned to one of these six categories with relative ease, even though there is a certain amount of overlap. As will become apparent, many authors have made contributions to several of the categories. And it could be argued that there exists an empirical or theoretical relationship between these groups. But the purpose of this review is to present current thoughts on *criteria* of positive mental health; not—at least, not yet—to inquire into the relationship of these criteria to each other, to an author's other contributions, or to theories.

One consequence of this emphasis on criteria is that similarities may appear where theoretical differences have not led one to expect them. Another is that it will be possible to examine these criteria from the point of view of mental health, rather than of the fruitfulness of the general approach of which they form part.

ATTITUDES TOWARD THE SELF AS
CRITERIA FOR MENTAL HEALTH

A recurring theme in many efforts to give meaning to the concept of mental health is the emphasis on certain qualities of a person's self. The mentally healthy attitude toward the self is described by terms such as self-acceptance, self-confidence, or self-reliance, each with slightly different connotations. Self-acceptance implies that a person has learned to live with himself, accepting both the limitations and possibilities he may find in himself. Self-confidence, self-esteem, and self-respect have a more positive slant; they express the judgment that in balance the self is "good," capable, and strong. Self-reliance carries the connotation of self-confidence and, in addition, of independence from others and of initiative from within. However, the terms have become en-trenched in everyday language in a manner leading to a large overlap in their connotations.

There exists also an overlap in meaning with other terms that indicate qualities of an attitude toward the self. Such terms are, for example, self-assertion, self-centeredness or egotism, and self-consciousness. These latter terms, however, have not been proposed as criteria for mental health.

A number of different dimensions or components appear to run through the various proposals. Those aspects of the self-concept that stand out most clearly are: (1) accessibility to consciousness, (2) correctness, (3) feeling about the self, and (4) sense of identity. Although not all of these com-ponents are made explicit by the writers who use attributes of the self as criteria for mental health, they are implicit in many of their contributions. Inevitably, there is a certain amount of overlap between these aspects.

Accessibility of the Self to Consciousness

In discussing attitudes toward the self, several writers refer predominantly to the breadth of content encompassed by the self-concept. For example, Mayman (1955), in speaking about the self-determining attitude, says: "An intact sense of selfhood or self-determination indicates a successful synthesis by the individual of all that he has been and done, with all that he wants to be and do, with all that he should and is able to be and do, without his disowning any major feelings, impulses, capacities or goals in the interest of inner har-mony."

In the course of his discussion of objectivity of self-percep-tion, to which we shall return, Gordon W. Allport (1937) indicates that the mature personality shows *"self-objectifica-tion,* that peculiar detachment of the mature person when he surveys his own pretensions in relation to his abilities, his present objectives in relation to possible objectives for himself, his own equipment in comparison with the equipment of others, and his opinion of himself in relation to the opinion others hold of him."

Both Mayman's and Allport's descriptions of a healthy self-concept include a large variety of content, such as actions, values, desires, obligations, and feelings in the past and present and in anticipation of the future. Clearly the quotations indicate that both authors regard a self-concept as desirable—that is, healthy—when it contains an image of all important aspects of the person. Mayman and Allport require awareness of the self in a healthy person.

Barron, on the other hand, appears to regard self-awareness as a counterindication of mental health (1955). He says: "We pay no attention to our self when we are in the best of health. It is when we are sick that the self comes to our notice. A person just *being himself* is not self-conscious. Self-consciousness arises from malfunction. . . ."

There is no necessary contradiction between the two views. Allport and Mayman do not stipulate that the self-concept must permanently dominate consciousness. There is in Allport's statement an important qualification (*"when* he surveys . . ."); and Mayman's "intact sense of selfhood or self-determination" may be close in meaning to Barron's "being oneself." Nor does Barron require that the healthy person be unable to be consciously aware of his own self. However, the juxtaposition of these views on self-awareness brings into sharp focus the fact that this criterion can serve as an indicator of mental health not at every moment but only when concern with the self is appropriate.

Kubie (1954) makes the point clearly: "[This does not] imply that in order to be healthy we must be self-consciously aware either of our every act or of our every purpose, but rather that the predominant forces must be accessible to introspection on need."

Correctness of the Self-Concept

The idea that it is good to see the self realistically and objectively is one of the most common in the mental health literature. Gordon Allport, in the passage already quoted, stipulates that self-inspection must be ɔbjective to be healthy. Such objectivity requires an ability for detachment. The temptation is strong to mistake what we would like to be for what we are. Cattell sees the *ideal self* as tending to merge with the *real self* (Hall and Lindzey, 1957). However, negative distortions of the self-concept are certainly also familiar in clinical settings. Whatever the direction, such distortion is based on an inability to control rationally the wishes and fears that thus color the perception of the self. It is in this sense that Fromm (1955) writes about mental health as characterized "by the grasp of reality inside and outside of ourselves, that is, by the development of objectivity and reason."

Feelings about the Self-Concept

The fact that each self, and presumably therefore each healthy self-concept, will contain some elements the owner will be, and others he will not be, proud of gives rise to the question of how he feels about himself. The most common proposal in the mental health literature is that he should *accept* himself—presumably his self-concept—including his shortcomings—*i.e.*, those elements of which he might not be expected to be proud. Maslow (1950) affords a typical example of this point of view:

Our healthy individuals find it possible to accept themselves and their own nature without chagrin or complaint or, for that matter, even without thinking about the matter very much.

They can accept their own human nature with all its discrepancies from the ideal image without feeling real concern. It would convey the wrong impression to say that they are self-satisfied. What we must rather say is that they can take the frailties and sins, weaknesses and evils of human nature in the same unquestioning spirit that one takes or accepts the characteristics of nature.

It is not clear whether Maslow takes the position that the healthy person does not experience ego-alien impulses or that his self-acceptance encompasses them too. His reference to sins and weaknesses suggests the latter interpretation.

In any case, he and others who emphasize self-acceptance are apparently referring to one's feeling about the total configuration of the self-concept rather than any single attribute of it. Presumably, recognized shortcomings are accepted in their relation to recognized strengths, and are realistically evaluated in terms of the possibilities and costs of changing the self.

Sense of Identity

Closely related to such balanced self-acceptance is another aspect of the self-concept which is frequently discussed in the mental health literature: the sense of identity. What Cattell calls the *self sentiment,* or what McDougall calls the *sentiment of self-regard* apparently refers not to any specific aspect of the self-image but rather to this integrative attribute of the self (Hall and Lindzey, 1957). They mean a global benevolent view of the whole self, a positive feeling that pervades and integrates all other aspects of the self-concept. The distinguishing mark of this aspect as compared to self-acceptance is its more cognitive emphasis on the *clarity* of the self-image. A healthy person knows who he is and does not feel basic doubts about his inner identity.

The sense of identity as an indicator of positive mental health has been particularly emphasized in Erikson's work (1950). He talks about it as the fifth stage in the development of a healthy person. (The preceding stages are basic trust, autonomy, initiative, industry.) Ego-identity, he says, "is the inner capital accrued from all the experiences of each successive stage, when successful identifications led to a successful alignment of the individual's basic *drives* with his *endowment* and his *opportunities.* . . . The sense of ego identity, then, is the accrued confidence that one's ability to maintain inner sameness and continuity (one's ego in the psychological sense) is matched by the sameness and continuity of one's meaning for others."

He contrasts this sense of identity with "a sense of *self-diffusion* which is unavoidable at a time of life when the body changes its proportions radically . . . ," here implying the close relationship between the sense of identity and the body-image. As a consequence of ego-identity, "real *intimacy* with the other sex (or, for that matter, with any other person or even with oneself) is possible. . . . The youth who is not sure of his identity shies away from interpersonal intimacy; but the surer he becomes of himself, the more he seeks it in the forms of friendship, combat, leadership, love and inspiration."

Most writers dealing with the sense of identity emphasize that its acquisition is the result of a long period of development, thus implying that a sense of identity is a suitable criterion for mental health probably only in adulthood, certainly not in childhood. Robert White (1952), relating his ideas to those of Erikson and Henry Murray, says: "There are many vicissitudes in the development of ego identity, but the overall trend is toward an increase of stability. . . . When one takes a long enough span of time, continuing well into adulthood . . . ego identity can be seen to become not only more sharp and clear but also more consistent and free from transient influences. It becomes increasingly determined by accumulated personal experiences. In this way it progressively gains autonomy from the daily impact of social judgments and experiences of success and failure."

GROWTH, DEVELOPMENT, AND SELF-ACTUALIZATION AS CRITERIA FOR MENTAL HEALTH

A number of authors see the essence of mental health in an ongoing process variously called self-actualization, self-realization, growth, or becoming. The idea that the organism strives permanently to realize its own potentialities is old. Fromm (1947) credits Spinoza with having seen the process of development as one of becoming what one potentially is. "A horse would be as much destroyed if it were changed into a man as if it were changed into an insect," Spinoza said. Fromm continues: "We might add that, according to Spinoza, a man would be as much destroyed if he became an angel as if he became a horse. Virtue is the unfolding of the specific potentialities of every organism; for man it is the state in which he is most human."

The term self-actualization probably originated with Goldstein (1940). He spoke about the process of self-actualization as occurring in every organism and not only in the healthy one: "There is only one motive by which human activity is set going: the tendency to actualize oneself." The idea is echoed in Sullivan's dictum, "the basic direction of the organism is forward," and it also dominates the thinking of authors such as Carl Rogers, Fromm, Maslow, and Gordon Allport. Sometimes the term is used as implying a general principle of life, holding for every organism; at other times it is applied specifically to mentally healthy functioning.

It is not always easy to distinguish these two meanings in the mental health literature. This lack of clarity probably has something to do with the controversial philosophical concept of Aristotelian teleology, to which the notion of realizing one's potentialities is related. The need for making the distinction in a discussion of mental health becomes urgent if one realizes that not only the development of civilization but also self-destruction and crime, from petty thievery to genocide, are among the unique potentialities of the human species.

Mayman (1955) is of the opinion that some of the proponents of self-actualization as a criterion of health have not succeeded in making the distinction. In a critical discussion of Rogers' use of the term, he says: "This position is insufficient in several respects: it presumes that this growth force is equally potent in all people; that if given the right of way, this force will inevitably assert itself for good; but most important of all it treats this force with almost religious awe rather than scientific curiosity. This urge to grow and be healthy is treated as an irreducible essence of life."

To make this life force an aspect of positive mental health requires that certain qualifications be introduced to distinguish its manifestations in healthy persons.

The process of self-actualization, as a rule, is described in rather global terms that make it difficult to identify constituent parts. Nonetheless, the various authors who regard it as a criterion of positive mental health seem to emphasize one or more of the following aspects: (1) self-concept (which has already been discussed and is mentioned here only to indicate the breadth of the term self-actualization); (2) motivational processes; and (3) the investment in living, referring to the achievements of the self-actualizing person as demonstrated in a high degree of differentiation, or maximum of development, of his basic equipment.

Motivational Processes

As indicated, Goldstein regards self-actualization as the only motive of the organism. Fromm (1941) seems to share this view when he says that the healthy individual recognizes that "there is only one meaning to life: the act of living itself." The qualification of this general motivational process, so that degrees of health can be distinguished, is more clearly made by Maslow (1955). He distinguishes deficiency motivation from growth motivation. Everyone, he assumes, has a need for safety, belongingness, love, respect, and self-esteem. Deficiency motivation serves to satisfy these needs; it avoids illness but does not yet create positive mental health. Growth motivation leads beyond such tension reduction to self-actualization of potential capacities and talents, to devotion to a mission in life or a vocation, to activity rather than rest or resignation. A self-actualizing person experiences the maintenance of tensions in these areas as pleasurable; he cannot be understood as being motivated here by the need for tension reduction. The greater the amount of growth motivation, the healthier a person is.

Gordon Allport (1955) concurs with Maslow's distinction. He says that growth motives "maintain tension in the interest of distant and often unattainable goals. As such they distinguish human from animal becoming and adult from infant becoming. By growth motives we refer to the hold that ideals gain upon the process of development. Long-range purposes, subjective values, comprehensive systems of interest are all of this order." He regards the dynamics of conscience as an example of growth motives.

Mayman (1955), too, suggests as one criterion of mental health the concept of growth and direction toward goals higher than the mere satisfaction of basic needs. Mayman calls this drive to change and development the heterogenic attitude. He contrasts it with "the immobilization of those patients who seem to prefer the security of their illness to the prospect of change, who seem not only to fear their own spontaneity, but even try to stifle this spontaneity. People with minimal evidence of the heterogenic drive seem to feel no wistful yearning for freedom or a richer life, but cling desperately to their imprisonment, like Lorenz's quasi-domesticated animals who refuse to part with their cages."

Mayman links this inner push toward new experiences to

Freud's life instinct: "We view the self-actualizing propensities of a person as aspects of the life-long cycle of growth and decline. They are expressions of what Freud has called the 'life instinct,' that set of forces which tends to upset established levels of equilibrium and move the individual toward new and more complex equilibria. . . . The 'life instinct' comprises all the impulses which tend toward pleasureful contact with others, synthesis and growth. These are the pressures which we presume to be responsible for the restless dissatisfaction with one's psychological status quo which we are here calling the heterogenic impetus.' "

Investment in Living

Pervading many of the passages already quoted is an implied criterion that mental health shows itself in a rich, differentiated life, involvement in various pursuits not restricted to what must be done for sheer survival. Several authors have been quite explicit on the point. Gordon Allport (1937), for example, speaks about the *extension of the self* as an attribute of maturity, describing it as an ability to lose oneself in work, in contemplation, in recreation and in loyalty to others. Maslow (1955) found that self-actualizing people "in general focused on problems outside themselves"; they have "feelings for mankind . . . a genuine desire to help the human race"; they are capable of "deeper and more profound interpersonal relations than any other adults"; they are "strongly ethical, they have definite moral standards."

Mayman (1955) formulates much the same idea as a process characterizing mentally healthy persons in speaking of their *investment in living;* by this, he means the range and quality of a person's concern with other people and the things of this world, the objects and activities that he considers significant. With such investment in living goes a "capacity to evoke an empathic, warm or compassionate response from others," he states. This observation is related to Maslow's finding that self-actualizing people seem to attract friends and admirers.

Lindner (1956) uses the term "employment" for this aspect of self-actualization. He describes it as "an attitude of affirmative dedication to existence, of profound and complete participation in living."

In Jung's optimistic psychology, "Self-actualization means the fullest, most complete differentiation and harmonious blending of all aspects of man's total personality" (Hall and Lindzey, 1957). Implicit in Jung's general formulation, and explicit in those of the other authors, is the notion that the healthy individual demonstrates concern for others and does not center all his strivings on satisfying his own needs. We shall meet this idea again in a later section.

It should be noted that the investment-in-living aspect of self-actualization can hardly be separated from its motivational aspects. Presumably the individual must be committed to these higher goals—concern with others, with work, ideas, and interests—and motivated to realize them, in order to achieve them.

INTEGRATION AS A CRITERION FOR MENTAL HEALTH

In the proposals suggesting certain qualities of the self-concept or self-actualization, or both, as criteria for mental health, there is as a rule, implicit or explicit, another criterion: this is generally called integration of the personality. Indeed, some writers clearly treat this additional criterion as part of either the self-concept or of self-actualization. Others single it out for special treatment. In view of its great importance to some, it will be treated here as a major category in its own right.

Integration refers to the relatedness of all processes and attributes in an individual. The coherence of personality, often referred to as the unity or continuity of personality, is an axiomatic assumption in much psychological thought. Indeed, psychological treatment of mental patients as a rule is predicated on the search for a unifying principle in terms of which the apparently most bizarrely inconsistent manifestations of personality can be understood to hang together. When integration is proposed as a criterion for positive mental health, something additional or different is implied. Some authors suggest that integration as a criterion for mental health refers to the interrelation of certain areas of the psyche; others, that it lies in the individual's awareness of the unifying principle. Still others imply that there are distinctions in the degree or strength of the integrating factor. And some are silent on this point.

Integration as a criterion for mental health is treated, as a rule, with emphasis on one of the following aspects: (1) a balance of psychic forces in the individual, (2) a unifying outlook on life, emphasizing cognitive aspects of integration, and (3) resistance to stress.

Balance of Psychic Forces

As a consequence of the psychoanalytic orientation of writers who speak about this criterion, it is formulated either as a specific balance of ego, superego, and id, or of unconscious, preconscious, and conscious psychic events. Earlier psychoanalytic formulations of health implied the exclusive domination of the ego rather than the notion of a balance between ego, superego, and id. Heinz Hartmann (1947) takes exception to this idea, which takes too literally Freud's programatic statement: "Where Id was, there shall Ego be."

Hartmann regards complete ego-domination as an unhealthy type of balance. According to him, the notion of a totally rational human being (*i.e.,* complete ego control) is a caricature of man, even though one takes for granted "the positive value of rational thinking and action for the individual's adjustment to the environment." His notion of the proper balance suggests an ego that can accommodate its corresponding id and superego and does not aim at eliminating or, perhaps, denying their demands. Thus he agrees with Kris (1936), who speaks of "regression in the service of the ego" as a preferred form of human functioning under certain circumstances, for example in the relinquishing of ego control when one wants to fall asleep.

Hartmann argues that rationalism is not synonymous with health, even though "it still plays a role where standards of health . . . are discussed. Thus it is often maintained that the freedom of the individual to subordinate other tendencies to what is useful for him makes the difference between healthy and neurotic behavior. Actually this is too small a basis to build upon it a definition of health. The ego-interests are only one set of ego-functions among others; and they do not coincide with that ego-function that also considers the demands of the other psychic systems . . . ; their prevalence in an individual does not warrant that the drives are harmoniously included in the ego, nor that the super-ego demands have been integrated into it."

Expanding on these ideas in another paper, Hartmann (1939) speaks of the plasticity of the ego as "one prerequisite of mental health. . . . But we would add that a healthy ego is not only and at all times plastic. Important as is this quality, it seems to be subordinated to another of the ego's function . . . a healthy ego must evidently be in a position to allow some of its most essential functions, including its 'freedom,' to be put out of action occasionally, so that it may abandon itself to 'compulsion' (central control)."

Here, the idea of balance is further modified. Not only does the healthy balance encompass id and superego, but the balance is changeable. Perhaps most of the time it is anchored in the ego; at other times the anchorage shifts to one of the other two systems.

Kubie (1954), too, sees the criterion of mental health in a specific balance of psychic forces; in his view, a balance among unconscious, preconscious, and conscious forces, with the unconscious reduced to a minimum. "The implicit ideal of normality that emerges . . . is an individual in whom the creative alliance between the conscious and preconscious systems is not constantly subjected to blocking and distortion by the counterplay of preponderant unconscious forces, whether in the prosaic affairs of daily living, in human relations, or in creative activity." This healthy balance will result in *flexibility:* "Thus the essence of normality is flexibility, in contrast to the freezing of behavior into patterns of unalterability that characterizes every manifestation of the neurotic process, whether in impulses, purposes, acts, thoughts or feelings. *Whether or not a behavioral event is free to change depends not upon the quality of the act itself, but upon the nature of the constellation of forces that has produced it. No moment of behavior can be looked upon as neurotic unless the processes that have set it in motion predetermine its automatic repetition irrespective of the situation, the utility, or the consequences of the act."*

The similarity between the approaches of Hartmann and Kubie is clearest in the former's emphasis on a changeable balance and the latter's emphasis on flexibility.

A Unifying Outlook on Life

A different tone and terminology is used by those who talk about integration on the cognitive level. Allport (1937), for example, speaks about a unifying philosophy of life as a sign of maturity. He regards this *unifying philosophy* as reconciling two otherwise conflicting tendencies. *Self-extension—i.e.,* losing oneself in the things of the world—and *self-objectification—i.e.,* looking at one's self with detachment—present an antithesis requiring resolution by an integrative factor.

Such a philosophy is not necessarily articulate, at least not in words. But a mature person "participates and reflects, lives and laughs, according to some embracing philosophy of life developed to his own satisfaction and representing to himself his place in the scheme of things."

Allport discusses several types of unifying philosophies. The first is *religion,* the "search for a value underlying *all* things, and as such . . . the most comprehensive of all the possible philosophies of life." There is also the *esthetic* philosophy, where the quest for beauty is the prime value. Allport views these outlooks as "autonomous master-sentiments that give objective coherence and subjective meaning to all the activities of their possessors' lives."

Apparently, the unifying philosophy of life results in the individual's feeling that there is purpose and meaning to his life. On a time dimension, the unity theme is presented by Allport as the intentions of the present which commit the individual to strive for specific aspects of the future. In *Becoming* (1955), Allport introduces a new concept, the *proprium,* for this integrating function. The proprium represents all regions of life regarded as central to the self and includes all aspects of personality making for inner unity.

Propriate striving distinguishes itself from other forms of motivation in that, however beset by conflicts, it makes for unification of personality. "The possession of long-range goals, regarded as central to one's personal existence, distinguishes the human being from the animal, the adult from the child, and in many cases the healthy personality from the sick."

Similar ideas occur in Maslow (1954), who speaks of the self-actualizers as "being the most ethical of people even though their ethics are not necessarily the same as those of the people around them," and in Barron (1955), who empirically found "character and integrity in the ethical sense" in persons judged to have a high degree of personal soundness. In both statements there is a clear implication that healthy persons possess a unifying outlook on life.

Thus, it is in the light of this aspect of integration—the unifying outlook on life—that the criterion of self-actualization becomes further qualified. The self-actualized person's investment in living is strong not because he was predestined to develop it but because he has a unifying outlook which guides his actions and feelings so that he shapes his future accordingly.

In the discussion of integration as a criterion for mental health Erikson's concept of identity, mentioned previously as an aspect of the self, must be mentioned again. In addition to the meaning of identity pointed out before, this master concept encompasses the balance of psychic forces as well as the notion of a unifying outlook on life. The former is clearly demonstrated where Erikson (1950) talks about the function of the sense of identity: "Psychologically speaking, a gradually accruing ego identity is the only safeguard against the *anarchy of drives* as well as the *autocracy of conscience.* . . ." And his concern with a unifying outlook becomes clear when he speaks of ego-integration (practically synonymous with ego-identity) as the crowning stage of development in terms such as, "It is the acceptance of one's one and only life cycle and of the people who have become significant to it as something that had to be and that, by necessity, permitted of no substitutions. . . . It is a sense of comradeship with men and women of distant times and of different pursuits, who have created orders and objects and sayings conveying human dignity and love."

Resistance to Stress

Those who discuss mental health as manifested in a particular response to stressful situations are actually concerned with distinguishing healthy from less healthy degrees of integration. The use of terms connoting behavior under stress—resilience, anxiety- or frustration-tolerance, and the like—leads to greater concreteness in specific criteria than does the use of the more general concept integration. Jack

R. Ewalt (1956) defines mental health as "a kind of resilience of character or ego strength permitting an individual, as nearly as possible, to find in his world those elements he needs to satisfy his basic impulses in a way that is acceptable to his fellows or, failing this, to find a suitable sublimation for them. . . . This resilience of character should be such that he can adapt himself to the vicissitudes of fortune, bouncing back to find new ways of satisfaction or sublimation after defeat. . . ."

Similarly, Wesley Allinsmith and George W. Goethals (1956) regard ability to withstand adverse events without inner damage as a criterion of health when they say: "When in conflict and unable to solve the matter rationally, the person has strong enough personality organization ('ego strength') or, as some would say, is 'secure' enough, to be able to stand the tension. A person with these characteristics is often spoken of as having 'frustration tolerance' or being able to 'delay gratification'; tension does not put the person into a panic."

All authors who talk about this aspect agree that tension, anxiety, frustration, or unhappiness occur in normal and in sick persons. The difference lies not in the presence of symptoms but rather in whether these symptoms can seriously unbalance the degree of integration an individual has achieved.

Thus Glover (1932) says, *"a normal person must show some capacity for anxiety tolerance."*

In an interesting empirical study on the behavior of patients under pre- and postsurgical conditions, Janis (1956) goes perhaps even a step further. Not only does the mentally healthy person tolerate anxiety without disintegration but, he suggests (at least by implication), the healthy person must be able to produce and experience anticipatory anxiety in order to cope better with subsequent danger.

Thus, the once popular notion that the absence of anxiety could serve as a criterion for mental health has fallen into disrepute. Whether or not one agrees with Tillich (1952), in his distinction of existential (healthy) from nonessential (pathological) anxiety, most authors in the field assume anxiety to be a universal experience. The individual's manner of coping with it is taken as the health criterion. Tillich thinks of self-affirmation and courage as the appropriate way of facing one's anxiety.

A NOTE ON REALITY-ORIENTATION

Three criteria—autonomy, perception of reality, and environmental mastery—share an explicit emphasis on reality-orientation. To be sure, this also has played a role in the criteria for positive mental health already presented. But as reality becomes the focus of attention, discussion in the mental health literature leads not infrequently into philosophical problems about its nature. This eternal question we wish to avoid. This is made easier by the fact that some relevant central and tangential aspects of this question actually are no longer controversial. The central aspect concerns the shift brought about by the development of modern science from a concept of *static* to a concept of *changing* reality. Says Wendell Johnson (1946): "No other fact so unrelentingly shapes and reshapes our lives as this: that reality, in the broadest sense, continually changes; once we grasp clearly what has been 'known' for centuries and what is, in fact, the central theme of modern science, that no two things are identical and that no one thing is ever twice the same, that everywhere is change, flux, process, we understand that we must live in a world of differences. . . ."

The tangential aspect of the philosophic question directly bearing on mental health—the dispute over whether there exists an essential hostility or a compatibility between man and the reality he is born into—no longer splits various schools of psychological thought into opposed camps. With the development of psychoanalytic ego-psychology and its conception of ego-forces and conflict-free ego functions as part of the native equipment (Hartmann, 1951), the psychoanalytic school has clearly indicated that it does not subscribe to the unqualified view of reality as hostile to man. Academic psychology, which long has accused psychoanalysis of just this sin, always has had room for aspects of reality both supporting and thwarting the individual's needs.

The positive aspect of reality as a pleasurable challenge and stimulation to the individual has recently been restated by Charlotte Bühler (1954). Taking note of psychoanalytic ego-psychology, Bühler says: "This concept of a positive reality would also imply the postulation of pleasurable activity ('function pleasure,' K. Bühler); that is, a pleasure in the stimulating process as such, not only in its elimination. Coping or mastery is from this point of view not identical with abolishment of stimulation, which is only one of two possible resolutions. Only harmful stimuli are mastered by way of elimination. The mastery of 'positive stimuli' lies in the integrative utilization of the organism's building process by means of which the living being becomes active in structuralizing material and imposing its own law on it."

The thought that the enjoyment of reality is good in itself is already embodied in the wisdom of the Talmud; it states that everyone will have to justify himself in the life hereafter for every failure to enjoy a legitimately offered pleasure in this world.

The emphasis on the positive aspects of reality is called for because, although the controversy has virtually been resolved on the theoretical level, it still lingers in discussions of mental health. Here the tacit assumption frequently still is that the world is fundamentally hostile to the individual. This may be the result of the fact that, historically, concern with health grew out of concern with disease.

The point has been raised here to avoid repetitive interpretation in the following sections. Unless there are good reasons to the contrary, we will assume that the authors quoted do not take an either-or position with regard to the relation of man to reality and that they are aware of the complexity of human experience in which positive and negative aspects of reality are not neatly separated.

AUTONOMY AS A CRITERION FOR MENTAL HEALTH

Many persons regard an individual's relation to the world as mentally healthy if it shows what is referred to variously as autonomy, self-determination, or independence. Most often, these terms connote a relation between individual and environment with regard to decision-making. In this sense, autonomy means a conscious discrimination by the individual of environmental factors he wishes to accept or reject. But occasionally autonomy is interpreted as a withdrawal from reality, as less need for the stimulation offered by the world, or as a small degree of involvement in external matters.

Expositions of the criterion of autonomy deal with one or both of two aspects: (1) The nature of the decision-making process, emphasizing the regulation of behavior from within, in accordance with internalized standards; (2) The outcome of the decision-making process in terms of independent actions.

Regulation of Behavior from Within

Foote and Cottrell (1955) describe autonomy as referring to "the clarity of the individual's conception of self (identity); the extent to which he maintains a stable set of internal standards for his actions; the degree to which he is self-directed and self-controlled in his actions; his confidence in and reliance upon himself; the degree of self-respect he maintains; and the capacity for recognizing real threats to the self and of mobilizing realistic defenses when so threatened." Hartmann (1947) speaks of "a general trend of human development, the trend toward a growing independence from the immediate impact of present stimuli, the independence from the *hic et nunc*"; and, somewhat later, of the "growing independence from the outside world, insofar as a process of inner regulation replaces the reactions and actions due to fear of the social environment (social anxiety)."

Mayman's description (1955) of what he calls the self-determining attitude avoids the connotation that autonomy manifests itself only when reality is threatening: "One's behavior should not be determined by external exigency alone, but dictated also from within, based upon that inner organization of values, needs, beliefs, accomplishments and still unrealized goals, which together comprise that individual's world view."

Independent Behavior

Maslow (1954) starts his description of autonomy much like Hartmann when he says it means a "relative independence of the physical and social environment." But he goes on to describe, not the inner processes which make such independence possible, but rather their consequences. According to him, autonomous people more than others "are not dependent for their main satisfactions on the real world, or other people or culture or means-to-ends or, in general, on extrinsic satisfactions. Rather they are dependent for their own development and continued growth upon their own potentialities and latent resources. . . . This independence of environment means a relative stability in the face of hard knocks, blows, deprivations, frustrations and the like. These people can maintain a relative serenity and happiness in the midst of circumstances that would drive other people to suicide. They have also been described as 'self-contained.'" Here there is a connotation that autonomy is a safeguard against the badness of the world, as if the only external events to be taken into account were those in conflict with internal standards and needs.

David Riesman (1950), on the other hand, explicitly recognizes that autonomy can manifest itself in going along with the world as well as in opposing it. In *The Lonely Crowd,* Riesman distinguishes various forms of characterological adjustment to the demands of society (tradition-directed, inner-directed, other-directed). These types of adjustment are different alternatives to the maladjusted, whom he calls anomic. The autonomous persons are those who on the whole are capable of conforming to the behavioral norms of their society—a capacity the anomics usually lack—but who remain free to choose whether to conform or not. Whatever their choice, they are less the creatures of circumstance than any of the other characterological types.

These conflicting interpretations of autonomy as a criterion of positive health are, perhaps, the result of contamination by another aspect of autonomy: not only how decisions are made and what consequences they have in behavior but also the content and aim of the decisions. This last aspect has actually been selected by Andras Angyal (1952) in his use of the term. Angyal describes the over-all pattern of personality functioning as a two-directional orientation: *"self-determination* on the one hand and *self-surrender* on the other."* Both tendencies exist in all persons.

The goal of the former, which he calls the trend toward increased autonomy, is "to organize . . . the objects and the events of his world, to bring them under his own jurisdiction and government." The goal of the latter "to surrender himself willingly, to seek a home for himself in and *to become an organic part of something that he conceives as greater than himself."* And later: "It is only in the counterfeit, the unhealthy behavior that one or the other of these basic orientations is partially obliterated; in a well-integrated person the behavioral items always manifest both orientations in varying degrees." Riesman's description of autonomous persons is compatible with Angyal's balance of the two trends.

At this point, the notion that mental health criteria have

an optimal, rather than a maximal, degree becomes particularly relevant. This idea, applicable also to other criteria and particularly to multiple criteria of health, has been proposed by M. Brewster Smith (1950). We shall return to it in another context.

PERCEPTION OF REALITY AS A CRITERION FOR MENTAL HEALTH

Pervading many efforts to conceptualize mental health is the idea that the way an individual perceives the world around him supplies an important criterion for his mental health. As a rule, the perception of reality is called mentally healthy when what the individual sees corresponds to what is actually there. In the mental health literature, perception is discussed invariably as social perception, meaning that the conditions under which perception occurs or the object of perception, or both, involve other human beings. This has an implication for terminology. Even if it makes sense under different conditions to speak of perception as distinguishable from other cognitive processes such as attention, judgment, and thinking, social perception cannot be so isolated. The term perception will here be used as implying various modes of cognition.

Two aspects of reality perception are suggested as criteria for mental health: perception free from need-distortion, and empathy or social sensitivity.

Perception Free from Need-distortion

At first glance the stipulation that reality perception be correct in a mentally healthy person appears so self-evident—

perhaps as contrasted with the psychotic's loss of contact with reality—that many authors present the criterion in an almost axiomatic fashion. Indeed, it is often treated as the *sine qua non* for reality adaptation. John Porterfield defines mental health as "that state of mind in which the perception of the environment, if not objectively accurate, is approximate enough to permit efficient interaction between the person and his milieu; . . ." (Ewalt, 1956).

Jahoda (1950) introduces correct perception as a criterion also in close conjunction with adaption to reality: ". . . correct perception of reality (including, of course, the self) may serve as another useful criterion of mental health. Unless active adjustment involving the modification of the environment is to rely on hit-or-miss methods, it must be based on correct perception of the environment." Maslow (1954) accepts the same position: "Recently Money-Kyrle, an English psychoanalyst, has indicated that he believes it possible to call a neurotic person not only *relatively* inefficient but *absolutely* inefficient, simply because he does not perceive the real world as accurately or as efficiently as does the healthy person. The neurotic is not only emotionally sick—he is cognitively *wrong!*"

Barron (1955), too, speaks of correct perception of reality as one of his criteria for mental health.

Yet there is a major difficulty inherent in this apparently self-evident criterion of mental health: it lies in the word "correct." Particularly when the object of perception is social in nature—but even when it is physical stimuli—who is to say what is "correct"? If one perceives a landscape in terms of form, another perceives it in terms of color, and a third in terms of both these or of other facets, who is most "correct"? Or, with regard to a social object, if a teacher sees in a child his limitations while another sees his potentialities, which one is "correct"? Correctness as a criterion seems to carry the implication that reality is static and limited and that there is only one way of looking at it. Yet seeing new hitherto unnoticed things in the world around us which, while they remain new, may appear incorrect to others, is certainly not mentally unhealthy in the opinion of the writers on the subject.

The point at issue here is that "correctness" of perception cannot mean that there is one and only one right way of looking at the world around us. But whatever the individual, and perhaps peculiar, way of perceiving the world, there must be some objective cues to fit the resulting percept. This is what accuracy or correctness mean when one speaks of mentally healthy perception.

To avoid the connotation that there is one correct way of seeing the world, the effort has been made to eliminate the word "correct" altogether from the mental health criterion and replace it by "relative freedom from need-distortion." The author uses this phrase in suggesting that mentally healthy perception means a process of viewing the world so that one is able to take in matters one wishes were different, without distorting them to fit these wishes—that is, without inventing cues not actually existing (Jahoda, 1953). To perceive with relative freedom from need-distortion does not mean, of course, that needs and motives are eliminated; nor that they have no function in perception. The requirement is of a different nature: the mentally healthy person will *test* reality for its degree of correspondence to his wishes or fears. One lacking in mental health will assume such correspondence without testing.

Parents, for example, ordinarily wish that their children will do well in school or fear that they may fail. A mentally healthy parent will seek objective evidence and accept it, even if it goes against his wishes. One lacking in mental health will not seek evidence, or will reject it if it is presented to him and it does not suit him.

As a mental health criterion, perception free from need-distortion reveals itself in a person's concern for evidence to support what he sees and anticipates.

Empathy or Social Sensitivity

Perception free from need-distortion is, perhaps, most difficult when the object of perception is a person—the self or others. The former has already been discussed as the correctness aspect of the self-concept. The latter, the perception of the feelings and attitudes of others, has been suggested as a separate criterion for positive mental health.

The major requirement of the healthy person in this area is that he treat the inner life of other people as a matter worthy of his concern and attention. Implicitly, he is also expected to arrive at conclusions about others that are free from distortion. Foote and Cottrell (1955) make this one of the ingredients of interpersonal competence, a term they use synonymously with mental health. They say: "People appear to differ in their ability correctly to interpret the attitudes and intentions of others, in the accuracy with which they can perceive situations from others' standpoint, and thus anticipate and predict their behavior. This type of social sensitivity rests on what we call the empathic responses."

It is perhaps worth noting that this criterion, although appearing quite rarely in the mental health literature, has received a good deal of attention from research psychologists. They have demonstrated by their errors and successes the enormous difficulties in discovering its presence or absence. This is a point one suspects to be true for most of these criteria, but there is evidence for this instance.

ENVIRONMENTAL MASTERY AS A CRITERION FOR MENTAL HEALTH

Perhaps no other area of human functioning has more frequently been selected as a criterion for mental health than the individual's reality orientation and his efforts at mastering the environment.

There are two central themes pervading the relevant literature: the theme of success and the theme of adaptation. As a rule, the former is specified as achievement in some significant areas of living; the latter is a toned-down version of the former, implying appropriate functioning with the emphasis more often on the process than on its result.

In the mental health literature adaptation and environmental mastery are treated on different levels of specificity. Ordering these emphases roughly from most to least specific forms of human functioning, these aspects can be distinguished: (1) the ability to love; (2) adequacy in love, work and play; (3) adequacy in interpersonal relations; (4) efficiency in meeting situational requirements; (5) capacity for adaptation and adjustment; (6) efficiency in problem-solving.

The Ability to Love

In at least one instance the ability to love is entertained as a criterion for mental health in the most narrow sense of the word—as the ability to experience sexual pleasure. Hacker (1945) says: "The biological concept as formulated by Reich appears to be by far the most logical because it is a medical concept of normality, derived from a theory gained by the study of mental diseases. It states that the attainment of full orgastic genital gratification is the only yardstick of normality for the individual. This does not necessarily imply that the sexual function is the most important one for man, though it recognizes sexuality as an extremely sensitive indicator of the personality functioning as a whole. The difficulty is to define what is meant by full orgastic pleasure in every instance."

It may not be amiss to point out that orgastic pleasure appears to be within the range of experiences open to the rapist and other sex criminals who, by such a criterion, would have to be regarded as mentally healthy.

But Hacker's paper, devoted to an effort to deal with the difficulty of defining what is actually meant by full orgastic pleasure, goes beyond it. Although he regards sexuality as the most sensitive criterion of health, he arrives at the conclusion that "the extent and form of integration in the total personality is the criterion; not whether one particular trend accords with current social views on sexual morality, or religious teachings. Full integration of the personality, the form and scope of which varies, according to the individual's possibilities, becomes the yardstick of normality."

Erikson's formulation with its emphasis on sexual gratification experienced with a *loved partner of the opposite sex* clearly meets the possible objection to a narrow view of sexuality as a criterion of mental health (1950). He regards sexual gratification as a sequel to the previously mentioned stages in the normal psychic development: "Psychiatry, in recent years, has emphasized *genitality* as one of the chief signs of a healthy personality. Genitality is the potential capacity to develop orgastic potency in relation to a loved partner of the opposite sex. Orgastic potency here means not the discharge of sex products in the sense of Kinsey's 'outlets' but heterosexual mutuality, with full genital sensitivity and with an over-all discharge of tension from the whole body . . . the idea clearly is that the experience of the climactic mutuality of orgasm provides a supreme example of the mutual regulation of complicated patterns and in some way appeases the potential rages caused by the daily evidence of the oppositeness of male and female, of fact and fancy, of love and hate, of work and play. Satisfactory sex relations make sex less obsessive and sadistic control superfluous."

Adequacy in Love, Work, and Play

Another group of authors regard environmental mastery as manifested in success in three crucial areas of living: love, work, and play. Ginsburg (1955) puts forward this proposition in the most direct manner: "My coworkers and I have settled for some such simple criteria as these: the ability to hold a job, have a family, keep out of trouble with the law, and enjoy the usual opportunities for pleasure."

Much of Alfred Adler's *Individualpsychologie* was based on the same notion. It is in keeping with the obvious importance of these areas of life that successful behavior in this respect enters into the mental health concept of quite diverse schools of thought. Mayman (1955) speaks of mentally healthy attitudes as contributing "to the formation of self-fulfilling patterns of love, work and play," and Blau (1954) describes the healthy individual as one who "is able to work adequately and to create within the limitations of his capacities, to relax after work and enjoy recreation. He can carry on his essential biologic functions of sleeping, eating, excreting, and so on, without any sense of disturbance or discomfort."

Adequacy in Interpersonal Relations

On a less specific level, a general competence in interpersonal relations is suggested as a criterion for mental health. Based on the theoretical and empirical work of Sullivan, Horney, and other neo-Freudians, the relationship to others is singled out as a criterion. Sullivan assumes that the major human goal is security resulting from satisfactory interpersonal relations. Foote and Cottrell (1955) build their concept of interpersonal competence largely on Sullivanian premises. They consider that "competence in interpersonal relations is a means by which members of the family are able to interact effectively in achieving their common ends and their individual self-expression and development."

A slightly different aspect of interpersonal relations as a criterion for mental health is among the eight items making up the World Health Organization's concept (Washington State Conference, 1951). There the statement is made that "the healthy person has the ability to be reasonably aggressive when the occasion demands. But he is free from any inner necessity to dominate other people, to lord it over them, or push them around."

Much in line with this notion are the views of the British psychiatrist H. V. Dicks, who regards "failure in human relationships" as the major reason for poor mental health, and "secure, affectionate and satisfying human relationships, . . . love and the elimination of hate . . ." as criteria for positive mental health (Ginsburg, 1955).

Following Erich Fromm (1941, 1947, 1955), a number of authors see the crux of the current mental health problem in man's alienation from nature, from himself, and from his fellow men. Mental health efforts must in their opinion be partly directed toward improving interpersonal relations. Rollo May (1954), for example, in his diagnosis of alienation in the modern world, describes it as a "characteristic of modern people in emotional difficulties . . . that they have become *alienated from their fellow men.* They have lost the experience of *community* . . . people really are afraid of one another. . . ."

Implicit in this statement of disturbance is the assumption that positive mental health consists in absence of alienation from others. But May does not spell out the positive aspect of interpersonal relations as a criterion of health. However, Dorothy C. Conrad (1952) gives an explicit statement of these positive aspects, after she has dealt with negative formulations. She stipulates among other aspects the following manifestations in the area of interpersonal relations. An individual shows positive mental health to the extent that he:

"Has positive affective relationship: The person who is

able to relate affectively to even one person demonstrates that he is potentially able to relate to other persons and to society. . . .

"Promotes another's welfare: Affective relationships make it possible for the person to enlarge his world and to act for the benefit of another, even though that person may profit only remotely. . . .

"Works with another for mutual benefit: The person is largely formed through social interaction. Perhaps he is most completely a person when he participates in a mutually beneficial relationship. . . ."

Meeting of Situational Requirements

One of the difficulties in arriving at criteria for mental health comes from the impact of the situation on behavior. As has already been pointed out, to speak of situations as healthy means stretching the meaning of the concept beyond permissible limits. Health refers to a living organism. The problem is particularly acute in the area of environmental mastery. Efforts at mastery will take widely differing concrete forms if we look at a child at home or in the schoolroom.

To do justice to these differences while adhering as closely as possible to concrete forms of behavior, a number of persons suggest that positive mental health is manifested in the individual's manner of meeting the requirements of a situation. These requirements have to be specially assessed for every situation in which mental health is to be judged. Fillmore H. Sanford (1956) does this, for example, with the school situation. He distinguishes three situational requirements: to establish appropriate relations with authority (teacher), with peers, and to acquire knowledge and skills. A child is mentally healthy to the degree that he functions effectively with regard to these three basic requirements of the schoolroom situation.

Other writers, too, speak of the efficiency demonstrated in meeting the requirements of a situation as a criterion of health without, however, specifying these requirements in detail. Julius Wishner (1955), for example, proposes that "psychological health and psychopathology be conceived as a continuum and defined in terms of the efficiency with which environmental requirements are met. For the present, however, this definition can be useful only in a relatively narrow laboratory situation because of the difficulties involved in the specification of objective requirements in the social sphere."

There is a troublesome implication in regarding efficiency in meeting situatonal requirements as a sign of health even when the requirements are specified, let alone when they are not. Some situational requirements, if met, can call for behavior that must be deemed unhealthy when viewed in terms of some other criteria. Severe deprivations, a harsh and demanding teacher, a prison, and the like, all may require behavior precluding self-actualization, autonomy, or perception free from need distortion. The implications pointed up by these examples are that the criterion be applied only when there is some consensus on the reasonableness of the requirement.

Adaptation and Adjustment

Those who discuss environmental mastery from the point of view of meeting situational requirements are either careful to spell out generally acceptable requirements or are in danger of assuming the invariable reasonableness of such requirements. Adaptation, with its connotation of modifying environmental factors, is not bound by a similar assumption. Here, there is no need to regard hard reality as unchangeable and only the individual as modifiable. Adaptation implies that a workable arrangement between reality and individual can be achieved by modifications of either or both through individual initiative.

From the psychoanalytic point of view, Hartmann (1939) has made the process of adaptation the focus of his discussion of mental health. He says: "Where many of the conceptions of health and illness . . . stand most in need of amplification [is] in the direction of the subject's relations with and adaptation to reality. . . . What we designate as health or illness is intimately bound up with the individual's adaptation to reality . . . with his sense of self-preservation."

Hartmann unfortunately does not discuss concretely the course adaptation might take. He does suggest, however, that "we often learn to find our bearings in relation to reality by devious ways. . . . There is evidently a typical sequence here, withdrawal from reality leading to an increased mastery over it. . . ." The article does not distinguish such healthy withdrawal from that of the mentally ill. Whether there is a fundamental difference, and, if so, what, is a question for research.

It is, perhaps, not an overinterpretation of his position to say that withdrawal from reality is one way of modifying it. That adaptation to reality is conceived by him as an active effort by the individual to choose or create an environment most suitable to his psychic conditions becomes clear when he uses pioneers and adventurers as an example: "The adventurer-explorer, the pioneer settler, and the man on the frontier are extreme but good examples of men maladjusted to their homeland who went out to find a new environment to which they could adjust."

The fact that this particular modification of the environment can legitimately be regarded as defensive has, according to Hartmann, nothing to do with its classification as healthy: "Nor does the distinction between healthy and pathological reactions correspond to that between behavior originating or not originating in defense. . . ."

It is true that the word adaptation is often used in mental health discussions synonymously with meeting environmental requirements. Hunt, for example, does so (Washington State Conference, 1951). He defines adaptive efficiency as the effective carrying on of the roles and tasks before an individual. The task before us, however, is not to settle differences in linguistic usage, but rather to draw attention to psychologically meaningful aspects in the mental health discussion. One such aspect is the idea that a healthy person can change his inner balance of psychic forces *as well as the external world*. This idea is conveyed by the term adaptation.

The idea is inherent in Freud's statements about the ego as an active agent: "[A normal or healthy ego] denies reality as little as neurosis, but then, like a psychosis, is concerned with effecting a change in it. This expedient normal attitude leads naturally to some active achievement in the outer world and is not content, like a psychosis, with establishing the alteration within itself; it is no longer *auto-plastic* but *allo-plastic*." Isidor Chein (1944) fully discusses the idea.

The term "adjustment" is actually used more frequently than adaptation, particularly in the popular mental health literature, but often in an ambiguous manner that leaves to anyone's whim whether it should be understood as passive acceptance of whatever life brings—that is, as meeting situational requirements indiscriminatingly—or as a synonym for adaptation. It might be noted that Jean Piaget's (1952) concept of adaptation is actually a synthesis or proper balance of the active and the passive component in man's arrangements with the environment. He calls the active component "assimilation," which means that the environment is made to provide the satisfactions one wants. The passive component is labeled "accommodation," implying that one learns to like whatever the environment has to offer.

Problem-Solving

One is again faced with two connotations of another term frequently used in the mental health literature: problem-solving. Some authors talk about problem-solving with emphasis on its end-product—namely, the finding of a solution. If such a criterion is applied to realistic life problems, it easily leads to the idea that success is the hallmark of mental health. In this sense, problem-solving meets the type of objection that earlier led us to exclude various states of well-being from further consideration.

Success is certainly a function not only of the individual's behavior but also of circumstances outside his control. To regard successful problem-solving as a criterion for mental health introduces an ambiguity in meaning, since success cannot be regarded either as an attribute of a person or as an attribute of his actions. Be that as it may, it may still be correct—and should be verified by research—that in our society people who are mentally healthy are more likely to be successful than those who are not.

The other meaning emphasizes the *process* of problem-solving rather than its end-product. In this sense, a case could actually be made that problem-solving is in many ways similar to adaptation or active adjustment. There are, however, differences in the usage of these terms which help to differentiate them from each other. Adaptation, normally a long drawn-out process, is one in which the individual can be engaged without being clearly aware of its occurrence, let alone its beginning or end. On the other hand, problem-solving can occur over both long and short time periods and is used in the mental health literature as presupposing a conscious awareness of a problem and an initial intention to deal with this problem. These differences seem sufficiently relevant to regard problem-solving as a criterion in its own right.

Whereas some persons make the assumption that the very fact that one is wrestling with a problem is a sufficient indication of mental health, others specify particular *modes* of problem-solving as criteria. The author's effort (Jahoda, 1953) distinguishes three dimensions of the process:

First, there is the time sequence of certain stages: awareness of the problem, followed by a consideration of means toward its solution, a decision for one or the other of the considered means, and finally the implementation of the decision. This sequence corresponds closely to several formal descriptions of the thinking process (Duncker, 1945). It is understood, of course, that in the course of problem-solving the sequence is usually less neat, with earlier stages being resumed in the light of subsequent ones, and often with all of them simultaneously in the mind of the problem-solver.

The second dimension is the feeling tone that accompanies the various stages. It is assumed that some discontent must be maintained in the earlier stages or, at least, that there must be an ability to delay gratification. These feelings serve as an incentive for proceeding to the following stages. Suppose a man experiences his current work situation as a problem. He intends to change it. But, as he faces the various possible ways of doing this, without proceeding to select one or the other, his intention dies out. He gets used to his situation. The likelihood is that he will not proceed to further stages of problem-solving. On the other hand, if he continues to maintain his intention and the appropriate feeling tone, he may follow such a mentally healthy mode as finding more suitable work. Here the appropriate feeling tone will be positive.

The third dimension of the process concerns the directness or indirectness with which a person approaches the root of the annoying experience. If he perceives his work as unsatisfactory a direct approach would lead to the consideration of other work; an indirect approach would consist, for example, of seeking substitute satisfactions in leisure-time activities.

The author suggests that a maximal degree of healthy problem-solving combines the three dimensions: a tendency to go through all stages, the maintenance of an appropriate feeling tone, and a direct attack on the problem. Going through this process, rather than finding a successful resolution, is taken as the indication for mental health.

IV

An Effort at Further Clarification

THE PRECEDING SURVEY of positive mental health concepts is encouraging in more than one way. The number of ideas is relatively limited; they can be reasonably well grouped under a few headings. In spite of diversified theoretical positions taken by the authors in the field, one gains the impression that there is among many of them a large overlap in meaning and intent when they talk about mental health; certainly, there are few, if any, contradictions between the various proposals. A case could even be made that several of them tap identical concepts on different levels of concreteness.

But, notwithstanding such encouraging features, the survey of the literature does not resolve the complex problem of clarifying the psychological meaning of positive mental health. Indeed, the review makes it quite clear that the least fruitful approach to the subject consists in assuming that anyone has *the* answer to the problem. We shall have to be content with recognizing that there are many tentative answers or approaches available and that none of them is as yet based on so solid a body of knowledge and facts that it can definitely be singled out as the most promising approach.

To say that there is as yet no entirely satisfactory approach available in the conceptualization of mental health is one thing. To conclude from this state of affairs that all further clarification has to await the results of empirical research is quite another matter. To be sure, empirical research is urgently required. Its success, however, will to no small degree depend on further clarification of some general ideas in the mental health field. Some of them will be discussed.

DIFFERENT TYPES OF MENTAL HEALTH

Since one obviously faces considerable difficulty in establishing systematic relations in the psychological content of ideas often expressed in poetic, rather than scientific, terms, the question arises whether there is not some merit in the diversity of concepts.

Perhaps the most cogent argument for accepting a variety of ideas about the nature of mental health is the recognition (Hartmann, 1951) that "theoretical standards of health are usually too narrow insofar as they underestimate the *great diversity of types which in practice pass as healthy . . .*" [ITALICS SUPPLIED]. If there are different types of health, is it not possible that at least some of the concepts discussed refer to such different types, and that they therefore need not, or should not, be brought to a common denominator?

Robert White (1952) illustrates the variety of points of views from which a person can be regarded as healthy. He bases his discussion of mental health and related concepts on the empirical study of "normal" people, meaning persons who have never needed professional psychological help to deal with the problems of living.

One of the persons studied, "Hartley Hale," was a physi-

cian and scientist of great ambition. He achieved mightily.
He was devoted to his work, successful and well-respected
in the profession. On the other hand, as a husband and
father Hartley Hale was less successful. Whenever work and
family life conflicted, he decided in favor of work. In which
area of life should one appraise his mental health? White
points out that different interpretations emerge when one
makes some, rather than other, aspects of Hale's life salient.
If one assessed Hale in terms of certain aspects of self-
actualization, he might be given a clean bill of health; if one
assessed him by his ability to "love, work, and play" he
would be judged lacking in mental health.

It could be argued that this is as it should be. And the
argument can be bolstered by an analogy with physical
health and physical illness. Apparently there, too, no single
concept has as yet been proposed. The medical profession is
content to operate with a variety of dimensions of physical
health whose relations to each other remain so far unknown.

The dimension of resistance to disease, for example, is
relevant to epidemiologists; it has no known relation to the
dimension of physical strength, a relevant health consideration among athletes and their medical advisors. Longevity,
yet another dimension of interest to medical science, may or
may not vary with the former. It is in this sense that William
Alanson White (1926) speaks of health as a relative notion:
"Disease and health are relative terms: in order to understand the nature of health and disease we must decide on
just how we are to approach the study of the human organism. . . ."

Neither is physical disease a unitary concept. As knowledge
advances, concepts which first appeared unitary are revealed

as comprising a variety of discrete notions; in a discussion of delinquency, Merton (1957) makes this general point: "This is not too remote, in logical structure, from the assumption of a Benjamin Rush or a John Brown that there must be *a* theory of disease, rather than distinct theories of disease—of tuberculosis and arthritis, of Menière's syndrome and syphilis. Just as classifying enormously varied conditions and processes under the one heading of disease led some zealous medical systematists to believe that it was their task to evolve a single over-arching theory of disease, so, it seems, the established idiom, both vernacular and scientific, of referring to 'juvenile deliquency' as though it were a single entity, leads some to believe that there must be *a* basic theory of 'its' causation. Perhaps this is enough to suggest what is meant by referring to crime or juvenile delinquency as a blanket-concept which may get in the way of theoretical formulations of the problem."

If one replaces in the above paragraph the word "delinquency" with the words "mental health," the appropriateness of Merton's statement is evident. Yet science does not stop at this point. Having dissolved an oversimplifying synthesis into independent aspects, a new and more systematic synthesis becomes possible. There is not one theory of disease. But medical research makes it possible to develop a theory for illnesses created by germs, for example. In the field of mental health, some believe that the dissolution of the "blanket concept" is the next strategic step.

To follow this strategy may bring an additional advantage. The idea has been expressed in discussions of mental health that people vary so much in terms of their native equipment that it is unreasonable to assume they could all be measured by the same yardstick. The genius and the moron as well as the average man may have their special types of mental health. There may be sex differences in this respect, even though industrialized society tends to even out some differences in the functioning of men and women.

But, ultimately, the adoption of different criteria of mental health for groups with different constitutional endowment is a question of how one wishes to look at such groups. For, as Kluckhohn and Murray (1948) have pointed out, every man is in some respects like no other man, in some respects like some other men, and in some respects like all other men. Those who speak of different types of health obviously prefer the middle position.

One way, then, of dealing with the relationship between the various concepts is to assert their possible independence from each other. They may designate various types of positive mental health. An individual may manifest mental health according to one concept but not according to another. A gangster may be judged healthy as far as his self-image is concerned; unhealthy with regard to meeting the requirements of a situation. Or, for that matter, William Blake, the mystical poet and painter, may score high in terms of aspects of self-actualization, low in terms of perception free from need-distortion.

The idea that there are several different types of health is not universally accepted in the field. To be sure, most writers clearly recognize that what they regard as the essence of positive mental health is compatible with a wide range of behavior and styles of life. They do not assume that one healthy person will resemble the next as one egg the other. But they regard such different manifestations as compatible with one concept of mental health rather than as requiring the assumption of diverse concepts.

If one accepts, however, the idea that there are various types of mental health, concepts in any one or all six areas may be worked with, and their relation to each other becomes a matter for empirical research, much as the relation between athletic strength and longevity is an empirical problem. But it will still be necessary to heed William White's request for deciding on just how to approach a study of mental health. There may be some who find it easy to select one of the many ideas which have been presented for practical application or research work. Others will hesitate to choose without further thought about what it is they are deciding for; with them, we turn to the next approach toward clarification.

THE MULTIPLE CRITERION APPROACH

When judging such a case as that of Hartley Hale, those who come to the conclusion that he is lacking in mental health are not necessarily blind to the positive aspects in his functioning. They may credit him with self-actualization, for example, but they regard this only as one element in mental health. He would be called a mentally healthy person only if he combined with self-actualization other healthy aspects, such as appropriate concern for interpersonal relations. In other words, they use a multiple criterion.

The relation of various components to each other in a multiple criterion can be understood in a variety of ways. Some authors regard a multiple criterion as composed of the various ways in which the underlying quality of mental health can manifest itself. Of this type, Maslow's idea of self-actualization is the outstanding example. A self-actualizing person not only is motivated to strive for always higher goals but also has an adequate self-image, is autonomous, creative, and spontaneous, has a reality-oriented perception of the world, enjoys love, work, and play, and has a well-developed individualistic ethic. In this sense, the multiple criterion approach is similar to the notion of a syndrome—as used in medicine, for example, when one speaks about the TB syndrome.

Another type of multiple criterion is presented, for example, in Erikson's developmental approach. It will be recalled that the various components of mental health that he specifies are each acquired in a definite stage of a person's development.

Allport's multiple criterion approach is of yet another kind. He combines various psychological functions jointly producing specified consequences: self-extension, and self-objectification, synthesized by a unifying philosophy of life, are necessary so that maturity can result.

A fourth type of multiple criterion does not assume a unitary cause or temporal lawful sequence but is empirically constituted. It is a cluster of related characteristics. Mayman, for example, assumes four components of mental health: the self-determining attitude, the heterogenic attitude, the alloplastic attitude and investment in living. The author, also a proponent of the multiple criterion approach—proposing active adjustment (environmental mastery), integration, and perception as jointly constituting mental health—suggests a different way in which these criteria may relate to each other: "It is easy to imagine social conditions which favor one or two but exclude others. Heroic efforts in fighting for a lost cause, for example, obviously exclude correct perception which, in self-defense, is replaced by illusions. Under conditions of unemployment active adjustment may be impossible. . . . Under the conditions of a polysegmented society with many incompatible values and norms, the unity of personality may be abandoned for the sake of opportunistic adjustment in terms of correct perception" (Jahoda, 1950).

According to this view, perception relatively free from need-distortion can be increased to the limit only at the expense of active adjustment. This multiple criterion approach to the concept of mental health would thus draw attention to the psychological price people may have to pay for developing one component at the expense of another under unfavorable environmental circumstances. In theory, of course, this *quid pro quo* idea of psychological functioning could also be ascertained if a variety of types of mental health were established and their antecedents and consequences investigated singly and jointly. In practice, however, such research might well be neglected unless the concept of health was so formulated as to make the question mandatory.

This idea has been elaborated by Smith (1950), who introduces the notion of optimum mental health, in contrast to other assumptions that every component of a mental health pattern could and should be maximized, whatever the psychological or situational context. Actually, he implies that the multiple criterion approach which uses components that can vary inversely with each other is based on an underlying unitary function which is available in a given quantity. If too much of the available energy goes into active adjustment, not enough is left for perception of reality. What the optimum combinations of components are under any given set of conditions he regards as a question for empirical research.

As one reviews these various ways of using a multiple criterion, it becomes clear that there is, of course, no incompatibility between the idea of diverse types of health and the use of such a criterion. Each specified type could be assessed by a combination of indicators. At the present state of our knowledge it may well be best to combine the idea of various types of health with the use of a multiple criterion for each. The former will prevent overgeneralizations; the latter will permit us to do justice to the complexity of human functioning.

MENTAL HEALTH AND MENTAL DISEASE

Early in this report, we committed ourselves to the idea that the absence of mental disease is not a sufficient criterion of mental health. The major argument presented at that time was that no satisfactory concept of mental disease exists as yet and that little would be gained by defining one vague concept in terms of the absence of another which is not much more precise. To reject this type of definition mainly on practical grounds disguises an issue of importance: the question of the relationship between health and disease. A few remarks on this subject are in order.

The traditional view that health is the absence of disease has recently been opposed by the idea that mental health and mental disease are qualitatively different. The point is most strongly made by Rümke (1955), who disagrees with the notion that "there exists between health and sickness an almost imperceptible progressive transition. . . ." In his opinion, *"The understanding of the disturbances of the sick man hardly contributes to the understanding of the normal man."* This formulation seems to deny how much general psychology owes to the study of the mentally sick as well as the possibility that increased knowledge of mental health may one day significantly contribute to the understanding of mental disease.

Yet, the idea that mental health and mental disease are qualitatively different seems to gain currency with many professional persons. It appeals to those who are puzzled by the existing evidence that similar pathogenic events lead to mental disease in one case but not in another; to those who are convinced of the organic nature of mental disease; and to those who are aware of similarities in experiences and defense mechanisms between persons who feel in need of treatment and persons who do not. Assuming that health is qualitatively different from disease, the extreme pole of sickness would be absence of disease; of health, absence of health. Such a view enables one to conceive of patients with healthy features, nonpatients with sick features.

Conrad (1952), for example, finds it useful to distinguish positive health from nonhealth as well as from negative health: "Positive health consists in ways of living that are beyond the frontiers of mere social existence implied by negative health. . . . This category (positive health) applies when there is evidence that the individual fully utilizes a capacity or is working in that direction." By negative health she means not pathology but some form of vegetating, without either positive health or disease.

To think of mental health and mental disease as two independent but contrasting conditions means to treat them as ideal types (in Max Weber's sense). As with every other typological classification, pure types do not exist. Every human being has simultaneously healthy and sick aspects, with one or the other predominating. The advantage of having established the pure types, and of conceiving of them as qualitatively different, consists in drawing attention to the health potential in patients and the sickness potential in healthy persons. Mayman, for example, has found this useful (1955). In his clinical experience, he has apparently encountered each of the four health components developed to some degree in various patients and has been able to use these health components as a lever in his therapeutic efforts.

It appears, then, that the definition of health as the absence of disease can be rejected on other than just pragmatic grounds.

What are the implications of this conclusion for the use of mental health criteria when dealing with the diverse disturbances which we call mental disease? In principle, at least, all the criteria are applicable to everyone, mental patient or not. Those who are professionally qualified to deal with patients are understandably more sensitive to the manifestations of disease than to those of health. It will take special efforts to introduce concern with health into clinical work with the sick. But such efforts may well be worth while.

The issue of the relation of mental health and mental disease is still exceedingly complex. Take, for example, the notorious judgment once made in a criminal case which held that "apart from an unshakable belief that he is the Messiah, the accused is perfectly normal." The statement offends common sense, inasmuch as this unshakeable belief appears to be a crucial disturbance in the man. But does it actually say anything but that there are sick features in an otherwise healthy person?

Or take the artistic production of mental patients. Some of Van Gogh's greatest pictures were painted while he was sick. Some of Hoelderlin's or Ezra Pound's greatest poems were created in an asylum. Some of Bruckner's greatest symphonies were produced while he felt under the desperate compulsion to count the leaves on the trees of Vienna's parks. Do such examples support the popular notion that you have to be crazy to be an artist or the equally widespread assumption that psychotherapy will eliminate extraordinary talent? Or can it be interpreted as an indication of a strong health potential among these artists who, in a different aspect of their personality, were also disturbed? Did they actually produce when in the full grip of a terrible disease or in the intermissions between attacks?

These and many other questions cannot yet be answered. The relation of mental health to mental disease remains one of the most urgent areas for future research.

THE VALUE DILEMMA

Throughout the preceding discussion we have attempted as far as possible to ignore one major problem, the problem of values. The postponement was deliberate. Hopefully, the discussion of values will profit from having first dealt with ideas of mental health in other contexts.

Actually, the discussion of the psychological meaning of various criteria could proceed without concern for value premises. Only as one calls these psychological phenomena "mental health" does the problem of values arise in full force. By this label, one asserts that these psychological attributes are "good." And, inevitably, the question is raised: Good for what? Good in terms of middle class ethics? Good for democracy? For the continuation of the social *status quo*? For the individual's happiness? For mankind? For survival? For the development of the species? For art and creativity? For the encouragement of genius or of mediocrity and conformity? The list could be continued.

Different persons will prefer different values and the criteria discussed here have differing relations to these values. A *prima facie* case could be made, for example, that meeting the requirements of the situation is more closely related to the maintenance of the *status quo* or to conformity than to creativity; or that the criterion of adaptation may automatically discriminate in favor of the economically secure who are in a better position to modify their environment than are those who live in less privileged circumstances.

The selection of criteria in terms of their relation to the high values of our civilization—or, for that matter, any other —seems so difficult that one is almost tempted to claim the privilege of ignorance. While it is easy to speculate about the relation of each criterion to a vast number of high values, we do not know whether such relations actually obtain. Does self-actualization really benefit the development of the species, as Fromm would claim? Is interpersonal competence a prerequisite for the happiness of the individual? Is happiness or productivity the value underlying an active orientation to problem-solving? Is altruism necessarily related to empathy?

Or, to put the difficulty of extricating the values underlying the selection of various psychological phenomena as criteria for mental health into a different perspective: How culture- or social class-bound is the value orientation of those who have suggested the criteria? Would people living in an Oriental civilization have considered contemplation and detachment as suitable criteria? Would the mental health label be more appropriately attached to self-assertive aggressiveness, to fit dominant values in the working class in Western civilizations?

Not only are the answers to these questions unknown; what is worse, there is no logically tight method of thought or analysis available through which the value implications of the various health ideas could be teased out with some degree of confidence.

There are two considerations, however, that help to reduce the value dilemma to one of somewhat more manageable size. First, we suggest that mental health is one goal among many; it is not the incarnation of the ultimate good. Second, the search for the values underlying mental health need not involve one in the megalomaniacal task of blueprinting the values for the distant future, or for all civilizations.

The discussion of mental health often makes, implicitly or explicitly, the assumption that a mentally healthy person is one who is "good" in terms of all desirable values. This assumption is, curiously enough, shared by proponents as well as opponents of the mental health movement.

People who are devoted to mental health work, often with an enthusiasm akin to religious fervor, see in it a panacea for all evil and all social problems or for the wholesale improvement of mankind.

The opposition against the mental health movement similarly assumes that mental health is suggested as the ultimate good. Humanists often oppose the movement because they fear that it will lead to a neglect of other high values. They ridicule mental health standards as incompatible with the appreciation of greatness, unique achievements, or the depth of human experience.

The assumption that mental health be compatible with all high values is actually not necessary. Human beings can never serve all the highest values simultaneously. To deny conflicts of values by setting up such global standards for mental health leads to a denial of the condition of being human. Only hypocrites or the inexperienced can assert that the choices in life are always between "the good" and "the bad." So simple an alternative is rarely posed. Conflict occurs in every life, and most frequently it is about alternatives good in themselves but incompatible with one another.

There are, then, other good things in life, apart from mental health. It is perfectly possible and plausible in these terms to maintain one's high admiration for William Blake, for example, and to regard him as not mentally healthy in terms of, say, reality perception. It is also possible for a teacher to specify as his goal that students acquire knowledge and to evaluate them in these terms even if the most brilliant student shows little self-awareness. Similarly, as we have seen in the case of Hartley Hale, it is possible to be an outstanding and devoted scientist without meeting the criterion of adequacy in love, play, *and* work or perhaps even of a balance of psychic forces. To consider such a person as lacking in mental health means neither condemning him to a mental hospital nor establishing his moral inferiority.

If this position is granted, all that is required from those working in the mental health field is to make explicit the values which induce them to select certain criteria, without aiming for the moon.

By way of an example, one value strikes us as being compatible with almost all of the mental health concepts discussed here: an individual should be able to stand on his own feet without making undue demands or impositions on others. Some such value underlies most clearly Ginsburg's idea that mental health consists of being able to hold a job, have a family, keep out of trouble with the law, and enjoy the usual opportunities for pleasure. Although this modest value is not as clearly implied in other concepts of mental health, it seems compatible with them. It appears relevant to different social classes, but whether it is meaningful outside the orbit of Western civilization is a moot question.

Others may feel that this value is not compatible with their notion of mental health, or that it is of too low an order; it is offered here only as an example—extricated from the literature intuitively rather than systematically.

Such a modest value premise takes the grandeur (and also the horror) out of the value preoccupation of the many mental health discussions that attempt to specify now the values by which the next generation shall live. Not that this task is unimportant or can be ignored. After all, whatever it is that a current generation does, it will inevitably affect what the next generation will regard as good. The experts in the mental health field have no special right to usurp this weighty decision. Politicians, humanists, natural scientists, philosophers, the man in the street, and the mental health expert must jointly shoulder this responsibility.

V

From Ideas to Systematic Research

To conduct systematic research in the area of mental health requires a translation of the ideas presented into concepts suitable for treatment by current research procedures. We now turn to the question whether and to what extent this is feasible.

The study of human behavior, like every other science, is based on observation. The purpose of all research procedures is to increase as much as possible the accuracy of observations. The crucial test for the soundness of research techniques is that several observers can arrive at similar judgments as the result of having independently applied the same procedures. To adapt the mental health concepts to these requirements means that the empirical basis for inferences about mental health, according to one or more criteria, be spelled out and that the conditions for the making of observations be explicit. Accordingly, we shall first discuss this question of empirical indicators for the various mental health criteria.

To establish empirical indicators—if it can be done—is only a first step in acquiring further knowledge about mental health. Neither scientific nor practical purposes in this field are adequately met by mere accuracy of descriptions. To understand mental health, and to apply such understanding, demands that the conditions under which it is acquired and maintained become known. The discussion of empirical indicators will, hence, be followed by some suggestions for seeking such understanding.

EMPIRICAL INDICATORS FOR POSITIVE MENTAL HEALTH

By and large, empirical indicators are not well developed in the mental health literature. As a consequence, the assessment of an individual in this respect is often left to the intuitive insight of an observer. The vast research literature on human behavior, on the other hand, presents many empirical indicators and ingenious devices for observation, but it rarely deals with the complex problem of what constitutes mental health.

The task before us is to attempt a *rapprochement* between these two fields. It would be foolish, of course, to attempt here a comprehensive overview of research techniques, let alone of the major unsolved problems in the science of man having intimate bearing on techniques for observation and measurement. All that can be done is to revert to the meaning of the major criteria and present selectively some research techniques which might do justice to them.

Inevitably, the discussion will touch upon some general issues and controversies in the study of human behavior; they will be identified where they first occur.

Attitudes Toward the Self

A variety of research tools and strategies for observation are currently available to deal with aspects of the self-concept. The basic design consists of a comparison between self-description and performance, or self-description and description by others.

Self-descriptions are elicited or inferred from relatively unstructured and unstandardized material such as autobiographical sketches or protocols of therapeutic sessions, from projective tests such as the Rorschach or Thematic Apperception Test, or from highly structured personality inventories and other paper-and-pencil tests, such as the Minnesota Multiphasic Personality Inventory or the Taylor Anxiety Scale.

Whatever the instrument used, the content of such self-descriptions consists of many different items: traits, motives, feelings, interests, or values. This raises a major question left unanswered by the mental health literature: Is every item referring to the self equally relevant for mental health? Take the accessibility of the self to consciousness: Is the awareness of what induced a passing mood as relevant as the awareness of what prompted one's choice of a marriage partner? And if not, which areas of the self should be accessible to consciousness? All? And what are these areas?

Or take the aspect of correctness of the self-concept: some studies have tested a person's ability to identify his own expressive movements, such as his gait, from a number of photographs. Is this a test of correctness of the self-concept? Or should mental health be inferred from the correctness of other features of the self-concept? And if so, which?

Or with regard to feelings about the self and sense of identity: Should pride in one's achievements be given the same weight as one's acceptance of grey hair?

All these questions point to the need for a theory which specifies dimensions of the self and their hierarchical relations to each other. They also imply that the mental health literature has insufficiently specified the concrete nature of aspects of the self that enter into calling a person healthy.

Depending on the characteristic of the self-concept under study, variations in the basic observational strategy are indicated. One way of arriving at a judgment about the accessibility of the self to consciousness, for example, consists of confronting a person with an assessment of his personality arrived at by competent observers. The person's reaction to such judgments may be acceptance, denial, surprise, or the like. These reactions then form the basis for evaluating the extent of his self-awareness.

Ingenious as this method is, it draws attention to two major problems, both of crucial concern to psychology. One is contained in the distinction between the self as it appears to others and the self-concept (the way the person sees himself). The distinction is akin to that between conscious and unconscious portions of the self, or the "real" self and the self-concept.

The other problem concerns the validity of assessments by others. However qualified an observer, however subtle his methods, is what he observes actually what he aims at observing? Applied to the self-concept, is the way the observer sees a person actually the way this person is? In scientific procedure the question is answered affirmatively if the observer makes a prediction based on what he has found and demonstrates the correctness of his prediction. He might state, for example, that a person who accepts himself as he is—other things being equal—will set himself achievable goals. Experiments can be conducted to verify this prediction.

But the mental health practitioner is rightly not entirely satisfied with this demonstration of validity. To make such predictions seems to him a relatively easy matter but not yet a guarantee that the observation, made under the very special circumstances of a research study, will be an indicator of what a man might do or feel under the pressures and influences of daily living. Since the practitioner is interested in mental health as manifested in daily experience, he occasionally becomes wary of research conducted in the rarefied atmosphere of a laboratory. In other words, he raises the question: Can research conducted under special conditions be generalized?

The question is crucial. Earlier in this report a distinction was introduced which has some bearing on finding an answer to it: the distinction between mental health as a more or less enduring attribute of a person or as an attribute of a specific action in a specific setting. It is generally agreed that we can know what people are only by inference from what they do. But every action is to varying degrees a function not only of the acting person but also of the situation in which he finds himself.

Scientific observation of human beings uses several ways of arriving at generalizations from specific actions. Perhaps the most frequent one consists in observing people under conditions that reduce situational influences as much as possible. One who takes a Rorschach test, for example, has no situational cues of what a "right" response is. In the absence of specific guidance from the outside, he is thrown back on cues from the inside. In this manner he reveals his personality predispositions. This is, of course, not entirely so. One might be frightened or attracted by the test administrator or pick out cues from his expressive behavior. No clinician, therefore, will want to rely on one test performance only for his personality diagnosis. But according to the theory underlying these tests, they present a good approximation of what a person is when relatively free from external influences.

Another way to approach generalizations about what a person is, beyond what he reveals in one concrete act, is to search for consistent trends in his behavior in a variety of situations. If a test score, a personality inventory, and clinical observation all indicate a well-developed sense of identity, the result inspires a greater degree of confidence that a personality attribute has been identified than when results differ in three situations.

Clinicians often approach the problem of generalization by making their inferences from a person's action in situations central to him. They regard the self as revealed in relation to a life partner as a better indicator of its actual nature than the self revealed while using the subway.

All these approaches are, of course, tenuous. But only an unrealistic perfectionist would look for more than an approximation in this area. Generalizations about an individual from behavior in one situation to that in another presupposes always that the psychological meaning of the two situations is understood. Where this is not the case, the psychologist will be as helpless in predicting as is the chemist when a substance he knows meets with one whose qualities are unknown to him.

To return to the self-concept: it is reasonable to assume that certain of its aspects will be more appropriately assessed under complex conditions. These are available for research through the use of therapeutic sessions dealing with the full complexity of life problems, in field experimentation and in special assessment situations that retain the flavor of uncontrived experience.

Growth, Development, and Self-actualization

To the extent that the mental health literature specifies this criterion, two aspects are distinguished: (1) motivational processes expressed in full utilization of an individual's abilities, his orientation toward the future and in differentiation, (2) and investment in living.

If one were to take these specifications too literally, an assessment of self-actualization might consist in establishing a person's abilities, comparing them to his actual work and leisure activities, and using the discrepancy, if any, as a sign of the degree of his self-actualization. By that token, a man with musical and mathematical gifts who becomes a great musician without doing anything about his mathematical talents would be judged lacking in mental health. But surely, this is not what those who suggest self-actualization as a criterion of health have in mind. Utilization cannot refer to all potentialities. Differentiation must be taken as occurring within one area of interests and not as synonymous with diffusion.

With regard to utilization of abilities, educational psychology has perhaps developed some concepts suitable for research. There, it has become customary to identify "underachievers" and "overachievers" among students. An underachiever is a student whose I.Q. would lead one to expect certain grades; his actual grades are below this empirically established expectation. In such a situation, the assumption is frequently made that the motives of the student are such that he does not give his best to schoolwork.

Other assumptions are possible and have to be ruled out before this situation can be used as an empirical indicator for the degree of self-actualization. When all the children in a class are underachievers, the teacher might be incompetent. A single underachiever may be motivated to utilize his abilities, but physical fatigue may prevent this. Nevertheless, the identification of achievement level in schools holds promise for the development of empirical work on self-actualization among children.

In other life situations, empirical standards such as are available in school are much more difficult to obtain. And intelligence is not always the best yardstick for evaluating achievement in life. It might be more in the spirit of the mental health literature to compare a person's ambitions and goals with the direction in which he is actually moving—that is, to replace the objective assessment of abilities by subjective goals, and to appraise these against the effort actually being made to achieve them.

Self-actualization is also expressed in a person's time perspective and in differentiation. Research techniques with regard to both are in a very rudimentary stage. Notwithstanding the fact that they play a significant role in Kurt Lewin's topological theory of the life space, empirical indicators have not been elaborated.

With regard to the other aspect of self-actualization, investment in living, some approximation of what the criterion means can probably be gleaned from time-budgets of a person. If one time budget indicates that an individual does little apart from what is necessary for survival whereas another is involved in his work beyond the requirements of a job, or is concerned with ideas, or is active in social relations, it is a fair guess that the second person has invested more in matters outside himself than the first.

But this is a very crude approximation. For we know too well that many activities and concerns are pursued not because they form a genuine link between the world and the self, but for purposes of self-aggrandizement, to escape other problems, to win approval, and the like. Such motivation indicates concern with the self rather than with object relations, as the criterion requires. The distinction between genuine and apparent concern with objects outside the self will perhaps be made easier once the psychoanalytic concept of "cathexis" is better understood and more amenable to empirical research.

Integration

Empirical indicators and research strategy are particularly difficult to suggest for this complex criterion. With regard to the balance of psychic forces it may be best to turn to the psychoanalysts who use the concept most frequently. Here a study of their modes of thinking may be the most promising next step. The goal would be to codify the way psychoanalysts transform the concrete data presented to them into the abstract notion of balance of psychic forces. What has been said about accessibility of the self to consciousness may perhaps apply when this balance is conceived of as a preponderance of preconscious and conscious over unconscious determination of behavior.

In order to arrive at generally applicable empirical indicators, it will be a wise precaution to use, in such co-operative research with psychoanalysts, material from patients as they appear after a successful analysis, rather than data from troubled persons only.

The assessment of a unifying outlook on life is complicated, and rightly so, by Gordon Allport's emphasis on the fact that such an outlook need not be an articulate philosophy. It is perhaps not too difficult to ascertain from prolonged interviews a man's basic tenets, if he can verbalize them. If he cannot, some sort of performance rating is indicated. Role-playing techniques might be useful for such efforts.

The empirical indicators for resistance to stress are more specifically formulated in the mental health literature. Anxiety- and frustration-tolerance and resilience are terms containing a clear directive as to the type of situation in which they should be studied: a situation presenting stress.

It is at this point, however, that we come up against another major theoretical problem of psychology in general: the problem of how to distinguish between the external stimulus and the experience of, or response to, that stimulus. To hear one's views attacked in a discussion may be experienced as stress by one person, whereas another may regard this as a pleasant stimulant. This same second man, however, may experience being alone at night in a dark wood as stress whereas the first man may deliberately seek out this situation. Should resistance to stress be observed when stress is subjectively present or when independent consensus agrees that stress has been imposed? In more general terms, the problem is known as the question of equivalence of stimuli. It has considerable philosophical and theoretical implications.

To the extent that research has been conducted on anxiety- and frustration-tolerance, the dilemma was avoided rather than solved by studying situations in which some correspondence between stimulus and experience was either directly ascertained or could reasonably be assumed in view of the intensity of the external stress. A case in point is the series of studies on resistance to stress in natural disasters, such as floods, prolonged isolation from other human beings, and the like (Chapman, 1954; G.A.P. Symposium No. 3, 1956). So are the previously cited study of anxiety and surgery and Clausen's (1955) study of wives whose husbands have been institutionalized for mental illness.

Similar situations offer strategic opportunities for the study of resilience. A crucial empirical indicator here may be the amount of time an individual needs before he can resume his usual patterns of living after change under the impact of stress.

Autonomy

The meaning of this criterion prescribes the situation in which observations must be made, namely, decision-making situations. Where the aim is to ascertain whether behavior is directed from within, it will be advantageous to use situations permitting alternative decisions, neither of which is encouraged or approved, on the assumption that the self-reliant person will be able to decide with relative ease and speed what suits his own needs best. Those lacking in self-reliance will find it difficult to decide and will search for external support.

Independent behavior, on the other hand, must be tested where some social pressure favors an alternative that the individual would not select if left to his own devices. Asch (1952) has designed an experimental situation lending itself admirably to this purpose.

Although the situational context for obtaining empirical indicators is relatively clear in this case, a number of other problems remain. Self-reliance can be demonstrated in choosing between coffee or tea or in making a vocational choice. Are both items of equal significance as indicators of autonomy? Independent behavior can show itself in the manner one dresses or in Luther's break with Catholicism. And, depending on many other factors, what is for one person an insignificant decision may be of great importance for another. We have met this difficulty already in discussing the problem of stimulus equivalence; what has been said there applies here too.

In addition, here as elsewhere, sensitive empirical indicators must be constructed so as to permit distinctions of the degree of positive mental health attributed to an individual. For this purpose a combination of various measures is indicated. The use of several observations which lead to a profile or a combined general score is a problem in its own right.

Perception of Reality

No other area in psychology has as long a tradition in experimental work, or has used a greater variety of observational strategies, than the area of perception. Yet the riddles of perception are far from understood and new techniques and ideas are pushing ahead the frontiers of knowledge. It is no wonder, then, that in research on perception most of the general issues and controversies in the science of man come to a head. Each of the general problems of research on human behavior mentioned before could be illustrated with reference to perception. We shall not, however, repeat them here. It must suffice to point out that the aspects of perception singled out by the mental health literature as criteria are intimately related to current research problems in perception.

Perception relatively free from need-distortion is a concept springing from the realization that although motives (needs) are always involved in perceiving, they are not, or at least need not be, the major determinant of the perceptual product. It also assumes that other cognitive processes—thinking, judgment, memory—are intimately linked to perceiving.

The situation for appropriate observations must be, of course, one in which an individual is emotionally involved with the percept in such a way that a distortion of its attributes would suit his inner needs better than the perception of what is. Perhaps the greatest difficulty here is the ascertaining of emotional involvement leading to a need to distort. Sometimes this need has simply been assumed without definite evidence. At other times, needs have been experimentally created. For example, persons have been deprived of water for some length of time and then been asked to identify ambiguous pictures. Those identifications having to do with liquids were taken as evidence of distortion. Tests of syllogistic reasoning have used the discrepancy, if any, between reasoning on neutral topics and reasoning on emotionally colored material as an indication that the emotional involvement created a need to distort cognitive processes.

The perception of the feelings and motives of others is appraised with the help of a strategy similar to that described for assessing aspects of the self-concept. A person's insight into the thoughts and feelings of others is compared with the latters' self-descriptions. The same tools for personality descriptions mentioned there can be used here.

The generality of empathy presents a special problem. One would like to know not only whether empathy transfers from one situation to the next but also whether it applies to understanding of all other persons or is restricted to special groups—for example, to people one likes or to people who are similar to oneself.

Environmental Mastery

Several of the aspects of environmental mastery are formulated in the mental health literature in such a manner that only the study of the full complexity of an individual's life history will suffice as empirical indication. Accordingly, data collection has to rely largely on case-study methods and therapeutic and diagnostic interviews, supplemented by time budgets and projective techniques.

The problems in this area arise mainly with regard to specifying the extent to which environmental mastery is a function of good or bad luck and to what extent it can be regarded as the individual's achievement. This means that the various case-study methods must not only deal with inner dynamics but must also pay attention to external events in their own right. Even though common sense alone would require such an approach, a surprising number of judgments of environmental mastery remain insensitive in this respect and engage in an unwarranted amount of psychologizing about hard facts. Such partial blindness is the result not only of overenthusiasm for psychological explanations but also of the considerable difficulty in sifting events provoked by an individual's inner dynamics from those occurring independently.

With regard to three aspects of environmental mastery— adequacy in love, work, and play, adequacy in interpersonal relations, and efficiency in meeting situational requirements —situational analyses are particularly important. What is needed here is research on what adequacy or situational requirements mean concretely. The conceptual approaches of sociology and cultural anthropology will have to be used toward this end.

Problem-solving is the one aspect of environmental mastery on which there exists extensive experimental research. The problems such experiments deal with are, however, mostly problems in logic or reasoning that in themselves are emotionally neutral. Further research will have to establish the extent that problem-solving tendencies, as demonstrated in dealing with these experimental tasks, have bearing on the approach to life problems. There is little doubt that some of the concepts used in such experimentation are relevant for establishing empirical indicators for problem-solving as a criterion for mental health. Duncker's concept of "functional fixedness," for example, refers to the tendency to use tools in the same manner in which one usually encounters them (1945). It may be as appropriate for describing approaches to life problems as it is for describing behavior under experimentally contrived conditions.

The accompanying chart summarizes what has been said

TOWARD RESEARCH ON MENTAL HEALTH CONCEPTS: A SUMMARY

KEY TO ABBREVIATIONS: AS: Assessment Situation. B: Behavior. CAM: Conditions for Acquisition and Maintenance. Co: Codification. CS: Case Studies. E: Elaboration. EI: Empirical Indicators. Ex: Experiments. Experimental. I: Inventories. Int: Interviews. O: Observation. P: Personality. PI: Personality Inventory. Pr T: Projective Tests. S: Self. SD: Self-Description. So: Sociometry. TB: Time Budget. Th Int: Therapeutic Interview. Val: Validation.

Current Usage in the Mental Health Literature

Mental Health Concept	Empirical Basis for Inference	Conditions for Observation
ATTITUDES TOWARD THE SELF		
Accessibility of the Self	SD of motives and feelings	When called upon
Correctness	SD compared to independent O	Observer's intimate knowledge of person
Feelings about the Self	S-evaluation; O of expressive B	O in various situations
Sense of Identity	S-eval., SD; O of group and role identification	O in various situations
GROWTH, DEVELOPMENT, SELF-ACTUALIZATION		
Motivational Processes	Utilization of abilities; future orientation; differentiation	Over long time period
Investment in Living	Interests outside S; object relations; concern with work, others, ideas, etc.	In daily life
INTEGRATION		
Balance of Psychic Forces	—	Psychoanalyst's intimate knowledge of person
Unifying Outlook on Life	—	Articulateness; in maturity
Resistance to Stress	Anxiety- and frustration-tolerance; resilience	In stress situations

AUTONOMY		
Inner regulation	S-determination in decisions; ability to take care of oneself	Availability of choices
Independent behavior	Nonconformity when appropriate	Social pressures opposing individual
PERCEPTION OF REALITY		
Perception free from need-distortion	Report of perceptual experiences	Existence of need; Val. of percept
Empathy	Assessment of others' thoughts and feelings	Social interaction
ENVIRONMENTAL MASTERY		
Ability to love	S report on experience of orgastic pleasure	Existence of loved partner; in adulthood
Adequacy in love, work, play	Meeting culturally approved standards	In daily life
Adequacy in interpersonal relationships	Existence of warm relation to another person	Social interaction in daily life
Meeting situational requirements	Behavior appropriate to situation	Assumption of appropriate standards
Adaptation and adjustment	Modification or selection of environment to fit needs	Over long periods
Problem solving	Combination of appropriate sequence of steps with appropriate feeling tone and direct attack on problem	Existence of environmentally created problems

Further Research Suggestions

Mental Health Concept	Available Instruments and Techniques	Considerations for Conceptualization and Design	Next Steps
ATTITUDES TOWARD THE SELF			E of Theory of Self
Accessibility of the Self	Th Int.		E of EI
Correctness	SD; I; AS; Th Int.	Val. by others. O of consistency between B and SD	CAM
Feelings about the Self	SD; I; Pr T; AS; Th Int.	Ex under stress; O of consistency between B and SD	CAM
Sense of Identity	SD or I; Th Int; stress Int.	Study variety of identifications. Val. of facts	Hierarchy of identifications; CAM
GROWTH, DEVELOPMENT, SELF-ACTUALIZATION			
Motivational Processes	Th Int.	Longitudinal studies	E of EI
Investment in Living	TB; CS; O; value and interest I	Val. of facts and motives	E of cathexis; CAM
INTEGRATION			
Balance of Psychic Forces	—	—	Codification of therapists' mode of inference for E of EI
Unifying Outlook on Life	—	—	E of EI
Resistance to Stress	O in natural and Ex stress	O before and after stress experience	Degree of stress specification; CAM

			Study decision-making
AUTONOMY			
Inner regulation	CS; Pr T; stress Int.	Open alternative	E of EI
Independent behavior	O; Ex pressure; AS	Definition of "appropriate" nonconformity	E of "appropriate" conformity, CAM
PERCEPTION OF REALITY			
Perception free from need-distortion	Int.; Ex created needs	Relation of percepts to cues	Relation of Ex to everyday perception; CAM
Empathy	Pl; Pr T.	Comparison of responses of judge and judged	Generality of empathy; CAM
ENVIRONMENTAL MASTERY			
Ability to love	Th Int.	—	CAM
Adequacy in love, work, play	TB; O; CS	Definition of "adequacy" and of situation	Study of culture standard and range of tolerated deviations; CAM
Adequacy in interpersonal relationships	So; CS; O; Pl; Pr T; Th Int.	Preferably not in contrived situations	E of EI
Meeting situational requirements	O; CS; Th Int.; AS	Definition of appropriateness and requirements	Sociological and anthropological study
Adaptation and adjustment	CS; Int.; Th Int.	Distinguish act from accident	E of EI
Problem solving	O; Int.; AS; Th. Int.	What is a "problem"? Equivalence of problems	Relation of Ex B to B in life

so far about the translation of mental health concepts into empirical indicators and presents several suggestions for further research.

SOME SUGGESTIONS FOR RESEARCH

Throughout the preceding discussion, two types of research questions have been mentioned. One has to do with technical matters such as the establishment of empirical indicators, the other with the advancement of substantive knowledge. This is not the place to go further into technical details; competent research workers must handle them empirically. These are not matters fruitfully advanced by speculation. Instead, we now turn to a brief discussion of some of the questions that should become answerable once the tools and techniques are available.

The Analysis of Mental Health Clusters

In the interest of economy of effort in research and practical application, perhaps the most urgently needed study is one of the interrelationship of the criteria. Consider, for example, the possibility that autonomy exists only when an individual has a well-developed sense of identity or self-acceptance, or that adaptation follows from a balance of psychic forces.

If a cluster analysis of the criteria would demonstrate such relations, the list of mental health concepts might be consolidated. A cluster analysis would have another advantage, too, that of permitting the establishment of a multiple criterion based on knowledge, rather than guesswork, about the relation of the components.

A word of caution is in order on the degree of generality that can be attributed to empirically discovered clusters. There is no reason to believe that the interrelations appearing in one case need necessarily be the same for every group. Differences in culture, social class, sex, or age may well express themselves in different clusters. Comparative studies in all these groups are indicated with regard to the frequency distribution of the criteria and their interrelations.

Mental Health Criteria for Different Age Groups

The study of mental health in different age groups is a research problem in its own right. In their current formulation, several criteria are applicable only to adults. Yet the need for mental health evaluation is just as great for children, adolescents, and the very old. Erikson alone among the various authors we have reviewed has given full attention to the maturational appropriateness of mental health criteria. To extend this concern beyond Erikson's formulation will require much research.

For example, the comprehensiveness and correctness of the self-image is a criterion of limited usefulness for children and young people. The rate of change in the self is undoubtedly much greater for them than it is at later stages in life, a fact that may easily lead to discovering apparent inconsistencies when the child is observed in various situations. What is more, self-description as a necessary tool for ascertaining aspects of the self is a task that may exceed the development of a child's cognitive abilities. To a lesser degree, the same holds for self-acceptance and the sense of identity. The latter, it should be remembered, is suggested by Erikson as a late step in a temporal sequence of development.

It may well be that parents and teachers, who are able to observe children continuously over long periods of time, could note possible indicators for growth, development, and self-actualization. However, as we have seen, the elaboration of empirical indicators in this category has not progressed very far. Much the same is true for the indicators of autonomy as applicable to children. Furthermore, the process of early education contains inevitably strong emphasis on curbing the child's autonomy. A minimal requirement for the application of this criterion to the behavior of children is identification of the areas in which autonomy must be curbed, so that they can be excluded as situations for gauging the child's mental health.

Perception of reality, meeting the requirements of the situation, and problem-solving are the criteria *par excellence* having meaning for all age groups, even though their empirical study will, of course, have to take age into consideration. Adaptation as the sense of actively selecting an environment to suit one's own needs is only occasionally open to young children in our civilization. To describe adequately the forms adaptation can take in childhood will require the elaboration of age-specific indicators.

Research in this area can be conducted from two points of view. Childhood can be regarded as a stage of life in its own right; in that case, clues for the establishment of criteria of health must come from what is known in child psychology. Or one can start with the model of the healthy adult and ask which behavior tendencies in childhood hold the greatest promise of health in adulthood. Taking extreme positions in this matter has led to the controversy between the proponents of "progressive" and traditional methods of education. This controversy continues to rage bitterly in the absence of facts demonstrating conclusively the impact of either method on the child or the adult-to-be.

Actually, the extremely child-centered approach to mental health criteria for this stage of life is as untenable as the approach regarding the child as a small adult. In the life of the child, present, past, and future shade imperceptibly into each other. The individual will function tomorrow according to the goodness and adequacy of his total equipment today. The next moment may deeply affect this equipment and it is reasonable to postulate that the nature of this effect will be to a considerable extent determined by the current state of affairs.

The mentally healthy child—healthy in terms of his age group—will be best equipped to deal with the subsequent events and thus with the gradual unfolding of the course of his life. But, however different the empirical indicators for mental health in childhood may be from those for adulthood, they must be conceived of as having a lawful sequential relation to each other. The need for research in this area is considerable. It will have to develop criteria appropriate for different stages in life and demonstrate how mental health in one stage leads to mental health in the next.

Research with Mental Patients

Another area of research concerns the possible application of these criteria to work with mental patients. Perhaps most immediately needed in this area are descriptions of the degree to which various mental health criteria co-exist with various types of disturbances. A systematic effort in this direction could lead to a series of other studies. For example, many efforts are currently being made to assess what progress or movement in therapy actually connotes.

The tranquilizing drugs apparently produce one type of effect. Many psychiatrists are of the opinion that the lessened anxiety and increased contact with others do not constitute a cure, but establish a condition making further therapeutic efforts possible. It would be of considerable interest to investigate whether the effects produced by the drugs, by subsequent psychotherapy, or both, are movements toward the mere elimination of symptoms of disease or toward the acquisition of health.

Other suggestions for the use of mental health criteria in the study of mental disease have already been made in a previous section. Their further elaboration should be attempted in close co-operation with psychiatrists.

CONDITIONS FOR ACQUISITION AND MAINTENANCE OF MENTAL HEALTH

There is ready agreement between all concerned that a full understanding of mental health demands that conditions under which it is acquired and maintained be specified. In order to meet this demand, research must single out some such conditions. And here the difficulty begins. A virtually unending number of conditions may affect the degree to which an individual possesses or displays any of the attributes constituting mental health.

Should one search for relations to genetic factors? Or biochemical processes? Does living in urban or rural areas make the difference? Or membership in a particular social class or ethnic group? Is it the standard of living or the level of

education? The geographical location or the physical qualities of one's home? Or the pace of life in the home town?
The composition of the neighborhood or the family? The
relation between mother and child or between child and
siblings? The early socialization process? Or a combination
of some or all of these factors?

For reasons of economy of effort as well as theoretical
elegance, it would be highly desirable to have some principle
available to help us sift these and many other possible factors
according to their psychological relevance for mental health.
The problem involved in the search for such a principle is
no less than the conceptualization of what is meant by
"environment."

This problem has challenged the great philosophers of
past centuries; it continues to challenge current theorists.
It is akin to the problem of distinguishing between stimulus
and response, between what is inside and what is outside the
organism (F. H. Allport, 1955).

Though the distinction between what is inside and what
is outside the organism is fundamental and clear-cut with
regard to objects, it is difficult to apply it to psychological
functions. Light is outside the organism; the visual nerve,
inside. Seeing, a psychological function, is equally dependent on both. In the sciences of man, the distinction is always
to some extent arbitrary. Even though various schools of
thought have made systematic efforts to deal with the relation between man and his environment, the great issue remains unresolved, at least to the extent that none of these
efforts provides a guide for choosing among the factors pos-
sibly influencing mental health.

In this situation a more modest empirical approach will

have to guide research on the conditions for the acquisition and maintenance of mental health. Here help is forthcoming in a variety of ways.

First, general consensus based on much empirical evidence holds that a crucial aspect of man's environment consists of those persons with whom he intimately interacts. For the infant and young child, the only other aspect to rival the human element in the environment may be his constitutional equipment. The fact that the infant lives in slum or palace, in city or country, in peace or wartime, affects him only to the extent that such conditions lead first to changes in his human environment. As the child grows, two important developments take place: he enlarges the radius of his activities, so that he directly experiences contact with objects, and his cognitive abilities develop so that aspects of the environment need no longer be physically present—that is, they can influence him via symbolic representation.

These processes of maturing infinitely complicate the manner in which the environment can affect mental health. The environment now can have an impact through a variety of channels. Yet new channels do not replace the earlier one; they supplement it. There is no way of saying with confidence that the mental health of a schoolchild is more crucially influenced by the personality of his parents, siblings, teacher, or classmates than by the fact that he is a Negro or lives in a rural area or comes from an educated family; even so, it is safe to say that the human beings around him are one crucial aspect of his environment.

A second set of conditions related to mental health is suggested by the results of interdisciplinary research. Psychiatrists and psychologists are more and more aware of the fact that certain regularities of behavior can be understood not only in terms of individual dynamics but also in terms of group memberships and identifications. Such regularities, the result of similar social conditions, lead them to be concerned with the wider human environment of a person as well as with his intimate human relations.

Collaborative research between psychiatrists or clinical psychologists on the one hand and sociologists or anthropologists on the other has demonstrated that it is worth while to extend the range of environmental factors in this way. Research teams, such as Faris and Dunham (1939), Kardiner and others (1945), Hollingshead and Redlich (1953), and Stanton and Schwartz (1954), have contributed to our knowledge of mental disturbance by identifying ecological, cultural, or class determinants. This approach could profitably be applied to questions of mental health. The newly emerging profession of social psychiatry and the establishment of therapeutic communities (Jones, 1953) are translating such research into practice.

A third approach to the identification of conditions conducive to mental health stems from the observation that man adjusts his behavior not only in interaction with other individuals but also in response to situations and institutions more or less independently of the particular individuals who happen to play a role in them. As one enters a drugstore or a theater, goes to work or to bed, a whole set of prescribed responses are called forth by the situation. Wright and Barker (1950) use the term "behavior setting" for locales having the attribute of eliciting largely standardized behavior. It is reasonable to assume that the behavior settings a person spends a good deal of time in will have a lasting influence on his psychic make-up. The school system a teacher operates in, or the specific requirements of any other occupation, present behavior settings of long duration that may significantly affect mental health.

A fourth set of environmental factors appears relevant for research on mental health. It is different from those already mentioned, inasmuch as it can apply to each of them as well as to many others. It is the factor of change in environmental conditions. It is a truism that environmental conditions change continuously and continuously provoke changes in the individual. Imperceptible changes are easily taken into one's stride. Sudden, major, or unexpected changes require a general reorientation. Constancy of environmental conditions, as much as frequent radical change, may be a good or bad influence on mental health. The direction of the change from "good" to "bad" conditions, or the other way round, may be as important as change *per se*. But there are some indications in the literature (Bettelheim and Janowitz, 1950) that one's sense of identity may be threatened, whatever the direction of change. In any case, the stability or instability of environmental conditions appears to be a psychologically relevant attribute of the environment.

In these directions, research on the conditions of mental health might proceed. There are undoubtedly others. Every serious piece of work in this field will have to come to terms with the fact that the various sets of conditions always exist simultaneously and that concentration on one or the other inevitably means a violation of the actual conditions of living. Those dissatisfied with this unending search for better and better approximations to an unattainable goal will have to turn away from science and seek elsewhere for their insight into the conditions for mental health.

VI

In Conclusion

At the beginning of this report stands a statement by Adolf Meyer contrasting two approaches to the field of mental health: the Utopian way, which leads to moralizing, and the scientific way, which leads to experimentation and deliberate action.

As one reviews the field of mental health more than thirty years later, he finds that no final choice between the two ways has yet been made. Today, too, there is a danger of mental health becoming a popular movement that lives by slogans and presents ten easy rules for being mentally healthy ever after. The final comment on the moralizing approach to the problems of living was made by the Austrian satirist, Nestroy, who made one of his most pompous characters say, "Better rich and healthy than poor and sick," and made him eloquently silent on how.

The present report should have made it abundantly clear that the complex problems of mental health will not be brought nearer to solution by exhortations. By far the most urgent need in the field is for more knowledge. Research is a slow and costly enterprise. It can fail. Or it can fail to be applied. However, in the long run, we do not know a better way to help policy decisions in the field than to strive for more and better knowledge about the conditions conducive to mental health.

If policy makers open the way to the acquisition of further knowledge, if practitioners in the mental health field cooperate with scientists in thoughtful experimentation, if the fruits of research can be applied without losing respect for the infinite diversity of human beings, concern with mental health may improve the quality of living.

VII

Viewpoint of a Clinician
by WALTER E. BARTON, M.D.

CONCEPTUALLY, it is difficult to see how a national program to reduce mental illness and increase mental health can be operated on any other base line than a straight one. In this continuum, illness is the point of departure and health is the goal. We work away from one and toward the other.

If we had solved, or even partially solved, the problems of preventing or treating major and minor mental illness, we could then justifiably concern ourselves with the issue of superlative mental health, or the degrees of goodness in good mental health. Unfortunately, we still have far to go in reducing illness. This is a practical concern, rather than a theoretical one.

We must recognize, of course, that Dr. Jahoda's purpose in this monograph is not to write policy for a national health movement, but to analyze and evaluate what different thinkers mean when they speak of mental health. Her concern is with the psychological—or, one might add, spiritual and intellectual—content of positive mental health. Such clarification is desirable. Dr. Jahoda has ably pursued the various theories about the psychological content of positive mental health and has shed a good deal of light on the issues involved.

Many physicians will find her approach a novel one. Some may instinctively oppose an approach divorcing health from illness as alien to their own understanding of health.

Dr. Jahoda's fundamental position appears to be that the absence of illness and the presence of health overlap but do not coincide. The physician, quite typically, I think, works on the basis that they do coincide, for all practical purposes. He sees health as the objective in the prevention, cure, or management of disease to the extent that he can help the individual avoid it, recover from it, or compensate for it.

The living organism so rarely presents itself, at all times or in all ways, in a complete state of biological, physiological, psychological, and—in sum—ecological harmony, and yet so characteristically strives for such a balance, that the clinician may still hold to his view that the absence of illness and capacity for achieving or restoring balance are consonant with sound health principles, as he must apply them. The pathologist at autopsy frequently observes so much pathology that he is far less struck that a patient died than that his diseased organs functioned as long and as well as they did.

All of us can benefit, however, from attempts to define and measure good health, whether psychological or physical, and should welcome heterodox efforts to do so. Perhaps, through the mind of social science, unencumbered by medical tradition, research may be designed that will eventually quantify the psychological content of mental health. The phenomenon of a superstate of good mental health, well beyond and above the *mere absence* of disabling illness, has yet to be scientifically demonstrated. We know little of it beyond occasional subjective, euphoric impressions of the subject that he is "bursting with good health," "feeling grand," or that "all is right with the world," meaning *his* world.

In contrast, the benefits of disease prevention and control have been tangibly demonstrated in increased ability to work and carry out social obligations, longer life, and individual morale.

Medicine has developed this useful way of looking at health and the normal to the extent that health as the antonym of disease has become a part of the philosophy, or tradition, of physicians.

The idea first was propounded by Hippocrates who held health to be a state of universal harmony, and the role of the physician to be that of restoring equilibrium between the various components of the body and the whole of Nature. This approach was encompassed by Walter Cannon in his principle of homeostasis, meaning a tendency toward uniformity or stability in the normal body states of the organism relating to the fluid balance and, more generally, the so-called "internal environment." By extension, the same idea of equilibrium permeates observation of such matters as "nitrogen balance" and various other physiological or biochemical states.

The inference of good health, or the normal state, as a manifestation of harmony or balance with the external environment can be found in biology as well as physiology. Out of Spencer's idea of evolution as the "survival of the fittest" came the notion of "nature in the raw" and eternal aggression and defense, which influenced the older conception of the germ theory of disease and made us appear victims of a kind of microbial warfare. But Darwin pointed out in *Descent of Man* that commonly in nature "struggle is replaced by co-operation." The concept of "a balance of nature" again emerged as a unifying idea.

In modern microbiology, the older idea of infectious disease as a "fight" against foreign "invasion" has been to a great extent superseded by the concept of man and his bacteria and viruses as habitually living together in various states of symbiosis or germ-host relationships involving infection, with or without apparent disease. Accompanying this has been a strong revival of the mutiple-cause theory of disease at the expense of the one-germ-one-disease viewpoint. René J. Dubos, for instance, regards "invasion" or "attack" as less characteristic of the relationship of man's pathogens to man than is "peaceful co-existence."

Subclinical or inapparent infection appears to be the rule, with periodic epidemics or individual imbalances due to lowered resistance of the human organism or heightened virulence of the microorganism actually occurring as exceptions.

So we see that a unifying concept of health and disease does run through medical thought, founded in biology and physiology as well as in biochemistry and microbiology. The tendency of the organism is to serve its structural, functional, and species purposes and, internally or externally, to strike some kind of balance that will permit it to do so. It is normal for the organism to do this.

Leston L. Havens (1958) has pointed out:

"Usually in medicine we say an organ is healthy if it does

its job within the normal range and over the usual time. We do not expect too much, although the usual range is not the range of the average man but of the average healthy man. Statistical norms are useful in this context and should not be dismissed despite the difficulties of agreeing on a normal population in the mental health area. Without such a point of reference, one cannot tell what is a toxic experience and what is normal tolerance. Without norms there is also the danger of unreal goals of treatment. This may be a significant clinical hazard. Ideal or even 'potential' health criteria are too easily spun out of theories or brief glimpses of people at their momentary best."

Both gross and cellular pathology have well-defined concepts of normal and abnormal. The tissue and cell are normal if they exhibit no disturbance of structure as compared to most tissues or cells of like kind. Precisely the same understanding extends from structure to function. Granted, the physician's estimate of what is normal sometimes has been of far too narrow a range, as for example in determining what constitutes abnormal blood pressure.

M. Ralph Kaufman (1956) sums up the issue this way:

"The organism and its relationship to its environment is in a constant state of flux which nevertheless involves a continuous series of processes utilizing all aspects of its functioning in an interrelated series of procedures aimed at the establishing of an equilibrium.

"The ontogenesis of the individual is of tremendous significance since within the potentials and limitations of the genus and species, the organism develops in a progressive and integrated way with each system (digestive, cardiovascular, central nervous, autonomic, psychic), shunting in, after functional maturation, to take over that role which its structure and function calls for in the total functioning of the organism. From the very beginning at the level of the sperm and ovum the processes have an adaptive equilibrium between organism and environment, each playing its essential role which involves the ultimate for survival. With the development and integration of the various systems, of which the psyche is one, the systems relate to each other in a kind of syncytium which means that no activity within one system can be isolated and unrelated to the total integrative, homeostatic, if you will, function of the organism. . . ."

Jacques S. Gottlieb and Roger W. Howell (1957) underscore the predominate note of disease prevention in the public health approach:

"The success of public health measures has been in large part dependent first upon the identification of specific important etiological agents and other variables in the illness process. It is like protecting our water supply against contamination with the typhoid bacillus or strengthening the defenses of an individual against a noxious agent as in inoculation with polio. This general technique has a certain similarity to the objectives of our previously described mental health goals; that is, removal of conditions of stress, of frustration, of deprivation on the one hand, (the etiological agent) while strengthening the ego defenses on the other (the inoculation). In the preventive program for physical illness this can be readily done, for the strategy is directed toward a specific objective. For mental illness, unfortunately, we cannot isolate a single variable, a single point of attack, but must be prepared to deal with multiple factors of etiological import. For prevention of physical disorders, success has come only after the knowledge of the etiology or of the important variables. For mental and emotional disorders, we may not have the knowledge as yet to really develop preventive programs."

Francis J. Braceland (1957) emphasizes the relationship of normal psychological development to disease prevention in certain situations. Rubella in the first three months of pregnancy may be a prologue to a mental defect in the child. Eclampsia may be a factor in cerebral palsy, or a metabolic disorder in a mother may contribute to the development of epilepsy in an offspring. Prenatal injury affecting later behavior is one possible consequence of poor maternal nutrition. Said Braceland:

"It is self-evident that increased alertness to these various possibilities would pay rich dividends in mental health, but the sad thing is that the psychologic aspect of such situations is not always kept in mind.

"Improved obstetrics, better use of protective services by all prospective mothers, the prevention of prematurity and its causes, and optimum care for the premature infant would cut the mental deficiency segment of our mental health problems by a sizeable amount. Multiple pregnancies, complicated delivery procedures, and stressful obstetric situations call for greater vigilance, as does the prevention of anoxia.

"The importance of diagnosing cretinism during the first year is of course obvious, in view of the good response to treatment at this time and the fact that later treatment will fail to overcome mental retardation. Steinfeld's hypothetical 'hunger trauma' in babies and its relation to later schizophrenia offers another challenge for prophylaxis. There should be joint obstetric and pediatric responsibility for fetus and infant and child, so that a clearer view emerges of the mental, as well as the physical, hazards of various complications from the time of conception and ways and means of combatting them. All of these things are important for the mental health of both mother and baby.

"There are at least three mental health problems which could be mitigated by more intensive development of existing public health emphases: the nutritional problems of pregnancy; the toxic deliria associated with certain vitamin deficiencies; and some of the confusions of elderly persons associated with both drug intoxications and malnutrition.

"Similar considerations pertain to infectious diseases which may directly damage the brain tissue. Encephalitis lethargica, even if so mild that it easily escapes detection, may result in mental impairment which, contracted in childhood, may be expressed in antisocial and irresponsible behavior. Inoculations against contagious diseases in children are essential to lessen the incidence of contagious diseases. Some of the formerly fatal cerebrospinal meningitides are now being restrained by antibiotics; unfortunately, however, we may be left with a defective individual requiring long and problematic rehabilitative periods. Early diagnosis and treatment of these infections is therefore essential.

"In adult life a psychopathic development may occur after brain damage, especially in the frontal cortex, the hypothalamus, and the midbrain. If cerebral contusion is at all extensive, it is likely to produce personality changes with neurasthenic, hysterical, or paranoid reactions, inadequate control of mood variations, and a general lack of initiative and energy. In the light of these observations we need to strengthen those features of environmental sanitation work which reduce the incidence of head and brain injury. These are a few of the areas in which good preventive and rehabilitative work may be done, provided that we are ever mindful of the close interaction of psyche and soma."

This summarizes what I believe is the typical physician's understanding of health. It is difficult for me, as a clinician, to separate the presence of health from those preventive measures that reduce the likelihood of the development of disease and illness. I believe most patients would settle for the absence of illness. If they are not sick, they are well. There would be no Joint Commission if there were no mental illness.

In this discussion, I have looked upon health as a product of disease prevention and treatment. It is proper, of course, for the scientific investigator to study behavior as a natural phenomenon, without a pathologic orientation.

The viewpoint I have expressed is tangential to Dr. Jahoda's discussion of the content of positive psychological health. Yet I feel sure she would agree that mental illness is the primary threat to positive psychological health.

References

Allinsmith, W. and Goethals, G. W., 1956. Cultural factors in mental health. *Rev. Educ. Res., 26*: 431.

Allport, F. H., 1955. *Theories of Perception and the Concept of Structure.* Wiley.

Allport, G. W., 1937. *Personality.* Holt, pp. 213, 214, 226.

———, 1955. *Becoming.* Yale University Press, pp. 49, 51, 68.

Angyal, A., 1952. A theoretical model for personality studies. In D. Krech and G. S. Klein (Eds.), *Theoretical Models and Personality Theory.* Duke University, pp. 132, 135.

Asch, S. E., 1952. *Social Psychology.* Prentice-Hall.

Barron, F., 1952. Personality style and perceptual choice. *J. Pers., 20*: 385.

———, 1954. Personal soundness in university graduate students. University of California Press.

———, September 1955. Toward a positive definition of psychological health. Paper read before American Psychological Association.

Benedict, Ruth, 1934. *Patterns of Culture.* Houghton Mifflin.

Bettelheim, B. and Janowitz, M., 1950. *Dynamics of prejudice.* Harper.

Blau, A., 1954. The diagnosis and therapy of health. *Amer. J. Psychiat., 110*: 594.

Boehm, W. W., 1955. The role of psychiatric social work in mental health. In A. M. Rose (Ed.), *Mental Health and Mental Disorder.* Norton, p. 537.

Braceland, Francis J., September 1957. Putting available tools to work. In *Better Mental Health,* Nat'l. Health Council.

Bühler, Charlotte, 1954. The reality principle. *Amer. J. Psychother., 8:* 626, 640.

Burgess, E. W., 1954. Mental health in modern society. In A. M. Rose (Ed.), *Mental health and mental disorder.* Norton, p. 3.

Cantor, N., 1941. What is a normal mind? *Amer. J. Orthopsychiat., 11:* 676.

Chapman, D. W., 1954. (Issue Ed.) Human behavior in disaster: A new field of social research. *J. Soc. Issues, 10:* No. 3.

Chein, I. 1944. The awareness of self and the structure of the ego. *Psychol. Rev., 51:* 312.

Clausen, J. A., 1956. *Sociology and the Field of Mental Health.* Russell Sage Foundation.

———, and Yarrow, Marian R., 1955. (Issue Eds.) The impact of mental illness on the family. *J. Soc. Issues, 11:* No. 4.

Conrad, Dorothy C., 1952. Toward a more productive concept of mental health. *Mental Hygiene, 36:* 456, 466.

Davis, K., 1938. Mental hygiene and the class structure. *Psychiat., 1:* 55.

Devereux, G., 1956. Normal and abnormal: The key problem of psychiatric anthropology. In J. B. Casagrande and T. Gladwin (Eds.), *Somes Uses of Anthropology: Theoretical and Applied.* The Anthropological Society of Washington, p. 23.

Duncker, K., 1945. On problem solving. *Psychol. Monogr., 58:* No. 5, 1.

Eaton, J. W., 1951. The assessment of mental health. *Amer. J. Psychiat., 108:* 81.

Eliot, T. D., May 1929. Standards of living, planes of living, and normality. *The Family,* 10: p. 87.

Erikson, E. H., 1950. Growth and crises of the "healthy personality." In M. J. E. Senn (Ed.), *Symposium on the Healthy Personality.* Josiah Macy Jr. Foundation, pp. 135, 138, 139, 141, 142, 143.

Ewalt, J. R., 1956. Personal communication.

Faris, R. E. L. and Dunham, H. W., 1939. *Mental Disorders in Urban Areas*. University of Chicago Press.

Foote, N. N. and Cottrell, L. S., Jr., 1955. *Identity and Interpersonal Competence*. University of Chicago Press, p. 55.

Friedenberg, E., 1957. The mature attitude. *Adult Leadership, 5:* 248.

Fromm, E., 1941. *Escape from Freedom*. Farrar and Rinehart, p. 263.

——, 1947. *Man for Himself*. Rinehart, p. 26.

——, 1955. *The Sane Society*. Rinehart.

Ginsburg, S. W., 1955. The mental health movement and its theoretical assumptions. In Ruth Kotinsky and Helen Witmer (Eds.), *Community Programs for Mental Health*. Harvard University Press, pp. 7, 21.

Glover, E., 1932. Medico-psychological aspects of normality. *Brit. J. Psychol., 23:* 165.

Goldstein, K., 1940. *Human Nature in the Light of Psychopathology*. Harvard University Press.

Gottlieb, J. S. and Howell, R. W., 1957. The concepts of prevention and creative development as applied to mental health. In Ralph H. Ojemann (Ed.). *Four Basic Aspects of Preventive Psychiatry*. State University of Iowa.

Group for the Advancement of Psychiatry, December 1956, *Factors Used to Increase the Susceptibility of Individuals to Forceful Indoctrination*. Symposium No. 3.

Hacker, F. J., 1945. The concept of normality and its practical significance. *Amer. J. Orthopsychiat., 15:* 53, 55.

Hall, C. S., and Lindzey, G., 1957. *Theories of Personality*. Wiley, pp. 96, 404.

Hartmann, H. 1939. Psychoanalysis and the concept of health. *Int. J. Psychoanal., 20:* 308, 312, 314, 315, 316, 318.

——, 1947. On rational and irrational action. In Geza Roheim (Ed.), *Psychoanalysis and the Social Sciences. 1.* International Universities Press, pp. 363, 379, 390, 391.

——, 1951. Ego psychology and the problem of adaptation.

In D. Rapaport (Ed.), *Organization and Pathology of Thought*. Columbia University Press, pp. 362, 373.

Havens, L. L., January 5, 1958. Personal communication.

Hollingshead, A. B. and Redlich, F. C., 1953. Social stratification and psychiatric disorders. *Amer. Sociol. Rev., 18:* 163.

Jahoda, Marie, 1950. Toward a social psychology of mental health. In M. J. E. Senn (Ed.), *Symposium on the Healthy Personality*. Josiah Macy Jr. Foundation, pp. 211, 219, 220.

———, 1953. The meaning of psychological health. *Social Casework, 34:* 349.

Janis, I. L., 1956. Emotional inoculation: Theory and research on the effectiveness of preparatory communications. Paper to appear in *Psychoanalysis and the Social Sciences*. International Universities Press.

Johnson, W., 1946. *People in Quandaries*. Harper, p. 24.

Jones, E., 1942. The concept of a normal mind. *Int. J. Psychoanalysis, 23:* 1.

Jones, M., 1953. *The Therapeutic Community*. Basic Books.

Kardiner, A., 1945. (With the collaboration of R. Linton, Cora DuBois and J. West). *The Psychological Frontiers of Society*. Columbia University Press.

Kaufman, M. R., September 27, 1956. The problem of psychiatric symptom formation. Paper presented before Michigan State Medical Society.

Klineberg, O., 1954. *Social Psychology* (rev. ed.), Henry Holt, p. 397.

Kluckhohn, C. and Murray, H. A. (Eds.), 1948. *Personality in Nature, Society and Culture*. Alfred Knopf.

Kris, E., 1936. The Psychology of caricature. *Int. J. Psychoanal., 17:* 290.

Kubie, L. S., 1954. The fundamental nature of the distinction between normality and neurosis. *Psychoanal. Quart., 23:* 187, 188.

Leighton, A. H., 1949. *Human Relations in a Changing World*. Dutton.

Lewis, A., 1953. Health as a social concept. *Brit. J. Sociol., 4:* 109.

Lindner, R., 1956. *Must you conform?* Rinehart, pp. 3, 205.

Maslow, A. H., 1950. Self-actualizing people: A study of psychological health. *Personality Symposia, 1:* 16.

———, 1956. Personality problems and personality growth. In Moustakas, C. (Ed.), *The Self*. Harpers.

———, 1955. Deficiency motivation and growth motivation. In M. R. Jones (Ed.), *Nebraska Symposium on Motivation*. University of Nebraska Press, pp. 8, 20, 24, 25, 27.

May, R., 1954. A psychologist looks at mental health in today's world. *Mental Hygiene, 38:* 1.

Mayman, M., 1955. The diagnosis of mental health. Unpublished. Menninger Foundation.

Menninger, K. A., 1930. What is a healthy mind? In N. A. Crawford and K. A. Menninger (Eds.), *The Healthy-Minded Child*. Coward-McCann.

———, 1945. *The Human Mind*. (3rd ed.) Knopf, p. 1.

Merton, R. K., 1957. Continuities in the theory of social structure and anomie. In *Social theory and social structure* (Rev. Ed.), The Free Press, p. 177.

Meyer, A., 1925. *Suggestions of Modern Science Concerning Education* (with H. S. Jennings and J. B. Watson). Macmillan, p. 118.

Milbank Memorial Fund, 1953. *Interrelations Between the Social Environment and Psychiatric Disorders,* p. 125.

———, 1956. *The Elements of a Community Mental Health Program*.

Mowrer, O. H., 1948. What is normal behavior? In L. A. Pennington and I. A. Berg (Eds.), *An introduction to clinical psychology*. Ronald, p. 17.

Piaget, J., 1952. *The Origins of Intelligence in Children*. International Universities Press.

Powell, J. W., 1957. The maturity vector. *Adult Leadership, 5:* 252.

Redlich, F. C., 1952. The concept of normality. *Amer. J. Psychother., 6:* 551.

Riesman, D., Glazer, N., and Denney, R., 1950. *The Lonely Crowd*. Yale University Press.

Rümke, H. C., 1955. Solved and unsolved problems in mental health. *Mental Hygiene, 39:* 183.

Sanford, F. H., 1956. Proposal for a study of mental health in education. First annual report, Joint Commission on Mental Illness and Health, Appendix H.

Shoben, E. J., Jr., 1957. Toward a concept of the normal personality. *Amer. Psychol., 12:* 183.

Smith, M. B., 1950. Optima of mental health. *Psychiatry, 13:* 503.

Stanton, A. H., and Schwartz, M. S., 1954. *The Mental Hospital.* Basic Books.

Tillich, P., 1952. *The Courage To Be.* Yale University Press.

Washington State Department of Health, June 1951, *Conference on research and evaluation of community mental health programs.*

Wegrocki, H. J., 1939. A critique of cultural and statistical concepts of abnormality. *J. Abnorm. and Soc. Psychol., 34:* 166.

White, R. W., 1952. *Lives in progress.* Dryden, p. 333.

White, W. A., 1926. *The Meaning of Disease.* The Williams and Wilkins Company, p. 18.

Wishner, J., 1955. A concept of efficiency in psychological health and in psychopathology. *Psychol. Rev., 62:* no. 1, 69.

Wright, H. F., and Barker, R. G., 1950. *Methods in Psychological Ecology.* University of Kansas.

Appendix

Joint Commission
on Mental Illness and Health

PARTICIPATING ORGANIZATIONS

American Academy of Neurology

American Academy of Pediatrics

American Association for the Advancement of Science

American Association of Mental Deficiency

American Association of Psychiatric Clinics for Children

American College of Chest Physicians

American Hospital Association

American Legion

American Medical Association

American Nurses Association and The National League for Nursing (Coordinating Council of)

American Occupational Therapy Association

American Orthopsychiatric Association

American Personnel and Guidance Association

American Psychiatric Association

American Psychoanalytic Association

American Psychological Association

American Public Health Association

American Public Welfare Association

Association for Physical and Mental Rehabilitation

Association of American Medical Colleges

Association of State and Territorial Health Officers

Catholic Hospital Association

Central Inspection Board, American Psychiatric Association

Children's Bureau, Dept. of Health, Education and Welfare

Council of State Governments

Department of Defense, U.S.A.

National Association for Mental Health

National Association of Social Workers

National Committee Against Mental Illness

National Education Association

National Institute of Mental Health

National Medical Association

National Rehabilitation Association

Office of Vocational Rehabilitation, Department of Health, Education and Welfare

United States Department of Justice

Veterans Administration

MEMBERS

Kenneth E. Appel, M.D.
Philadelphia, Pa.

Walter H. Baer, M.D.
Peoria, Illinois

Leo H. Bartemeier, M.D.
Baltimore, Maryland

Walter E. Barton, M.D.
Boston, Massachusetts

Otto L. Bettag, M.D.
Springfield, Illinois

Mr. George Bingaman
Purcell, Oklahoma

Kathleen Black, R.N.
New York, New York

Daniel Blain, M.D.
Washington, D.C.

Francis J. Braceland, M.D.
Hartford, Connecticut

Hugh T. Carmichael, M.D.
Chicago, Illinois

J. Frank Casey, M.D.
Washington, D.C.

James M. Cunningham, M.D.
Dayton, Ohio

John E. Davis, Sc.D.
Rehoboth Beach, Delaware

Neil A. Dayton, M.D.
Mansfield Depot, Conn.

Miss Loula Dunn
Chicago, Illinois

Howard D. Fabing, M.D.
Cincinnati, Ohio

Rev. Patrick J. Frawley, Ph.D.
New York, New York

Mr. Mike Gorman
Washington, D.C.

Robert T. Hewitt, M.D.
Bethesda, Maryland

Herman E. Hilleboe, M.D.
Albany, New York

Nicholas Hobbs, Ph.D.
Nashville, Tennessee

Bartholomew W. Hogan, Rear
Adm. M.C., U.S.N., Washington, D.C.

Louis Jacobs, M.D.
Washington, D.C.

M. Ralph Kaufman, M.D.
New York, New York

William S. Langford, M.D.
New York, New York

Miss Madeleine Lay
New York, New York

Jack Masur, M.D.
Bethesda, Maryland

Berwyn F. Mattison, M.D.
New York, New York

Ernst Mayr, Ph.D.
Cambridge, Mass.

Robert T. Morse, M.D.
Washington, D.C.

Ralph H. Ojemann, Ph.D.
Iowa City, Iowa

Winfred Overholser, M.D.
Washington, D.C.

Howard W. Potter, M.D.
New York, New York

Mr. Charles Schlaifer
New York, New York

Lauren H. Smith, M.D.
Philadelphia, Pa.

M. Brewster Smith, Ph.D.
New York, New York

Mr. Sidney Spector
Chicago, Illinois

Mesrop A. Tarumianz, M.D.
Farnhurst, Delaware

David W. Tiedman, Ed.D.
Cambridge, Mass.

Harvey J. Tompkins, M.D.
New York, New York

Beatrice D. Wade, O.T.R.
Chicago, Illinois

Mr. E. B. Whitten
Washington, D.C.

Helen Witmer, Ph.D.
Washington, D.C.

Luther E. Woodward, Ph.D.
New York, New York

Index

A

accommodation, 62

achievement level, as measure of self-actualization, 87-88

acquisition of mental health, 104

adaptation
problem-solving and, 63
reality and, 60-62
(*see also* environmental mastery)

adjustment
adaptation and, 62-63
to environment, autonomy and, 47-48

Adler, Alfred, 55

age groups, mental health criteria and, 101-103

Alexander, Franz, 12

alienation, 57

Allinsmith, Wesley, 42

alloplastic attitude, 71

Allport, F. H., 105

Allport, Gordon W., 25-26, 27, 31, 33, 34, 39-40, 71, 90

Angyal, Andras, 48

anthropology

mental disease and, 12-14
normality and, 15

anxiety, 42-43

anxiety tolerance, 41-43
measurement of, 90-91
(*see also* stress)

Asch, S. E., 14, 92

assessment, of mental health, 81-100

assimilation, 62

attitude
alloplastic, 71
heterogenic, 33-34
(*see also* self, attitude toward)

autonomy, 23, 43, 45-49, 71
measurement of, 91-92

B

Barker, R. G., 107

Barron, F., 26, 40, 50

Barton, Walter E., 111-119

becoming (*see* self-actualization)

Benedict, Ruth, 12

Bettelheim, B., 108

Blau, A., 56

Boehm, W. W., 19, 20

Braceland, Francis J., 117-119

SOCIAL SCIENCE LIBRARY

Manor Road Building
Manor Road
Oxford OX1 3UQ
Tel: (2)71093 (enquiries and renewals)
http://www.ssl.ox.ac.uk

This is a NORMAL LOAN item.

We will email you a reminder before this item is due.

Please see http://www.ssl.ox.ac.uk/lending.html
for details on:

- loan policies; these are also displayed on the notice boards and in our library guide.

- how to check when your books are due back.

- how to renew your books, including information on the maximum number of renewals. Items may be renewed if not reserved by another reader. Items must be renewed before the library closes on the due date.

- level of fines; fines are charged on overdue books.

Please note that this item may be recalled during Term.